Mark Diacono is lucky enough to spend most of his time eating, growing, writing and talking about food.

He is an award-winning writer and photographer and has written and/or photographed thirteen books, including *A Year at Otter Farm* (André Simon Food Book of the Year 2014), *A Taste of the Unexpected* (Guild of Food Writers' Food Book of the Year 2011), *The New Kitchen Garden* (Garden Media Guild Book of the Year 2015), and his most recent book, *Sour*.

His refreshing approach to growing unusual and forgotten food along with the best of the familiar has done much to inspire a new generation of gardeners and cooks. As well as his books, Mark has written for the weekend broadsheets, and magazines as diverse as *National Geographic*, *Country Life* and *Delicious*.

Mark was involved with River Cottage in the early days, appearing in the TV series and writing three of the *River Cottage Handbook* series.

Twitter: @MarkDiacono

Instagram: @mark_diacono

GROW & COOK

The Ultimate Kitchen Garden Guide

MARK DIACONO

For my Mum

Copyright © Mark Diacono 2015

Illustrations copyright © Clover Robin 2019

The right of Mark Diacono to be identified as the Author of
the Work has been asserted by him in accordance with the
Copyright, Designs and Patents Act 1988.

First published in 2015 as THE NEW KITCHEN GARDEN by Saltyard Books
An imprint of John Murray Publishers

First published in paperback in 2020 as GROW & COOK by Headline Home
An imprint of Headline Publishing Group

1

Cataloguing in Publication Data is available from the British Library

ISBN 978 1 4722 6546 3
eISBN 978 1 4722 7017 7

Designed and typeset by EM&EN
Printed and bound in Great Britain by Clays Ltd, Elcograf S.p.A.

Headline's policy is to use papers that are natural, renewable and recyclable
products and made from wood grown in well-managed forests and other
controlled sources. The logging and manufacturing processes are expected
to conform to the environmental regulations of the country of origin.

MIX
Paper from
responsible sources
FSC® C104740
www.fsc.org

HEADLINE PUBLISHING GROUP
An Hachette UK Company
Carmelite House
50 Victoria Embankment
London
EC4Y 0DZ

www.headline.co.uk
www.hachette.co.uk

CONTENTS

INTRODUCTION

Grow at least a little of what you eat, just once. You deserve it. Life is busy, I know, and time is precious, but don't let too much time pass before you taste a sun-warmed tomato plucked from a plant you grew yourself; before you enjoy a salad of homegrown leaves; or know the pleasure of an apple, a peach or a handful of strawberries eaten straight from the plant. Even if you do it only once, it will enrich your fleeting time on this planet. You don't even need to commit to an allotment or a garden: create a collection of herbs by the door and though they ask little of you, they can change every meal you eat.

Look over a few garden walls or into an allotment and you'll see that most of the space given over to edibles is dedicated to a few familiar foods. Potatoes, carrots, onions, various cabbages and salad leaves dominate, and very fine they are too. And yet they are a slender selection from the many possibilities for your kitchen garden. This book is an encouragement to take a wider look, to consider *all* the finest flavours I know. Whether your garden is a bunch of containers, a small patch of earth, a forest garden or a smallholding, you'll find a wealth of delicious possibilities from which to choose.

To get the most from your garden, let go of all preconceptions of what you might grow. Imagine no one had ever grown any of their own food, and that an all-powerful deity appeared in the sky and bestowed upon each of us a little outdoor space in which we may grow anything we'd like to eat. Faced with all this beautiful possibility – the prospect of our favourite flavours and textures, of tastes and experiences we may never have tried but that take our fancy, and only the climate and our imagination to limit us – what would you choose to grow?

I'm optimistic enough to think it unlikely that, fuelled by the excitement and freshness of new possibilities, we would dedicate most of our garden to the cheapest, most disease-prone, most widely available food there is. With a clean mental slate and no history of gardening to dominate our thinking, we would almost certainly come up with different choices to our neighbours. I love sprouts, No. 46 loathes them; the family over the road wants a mini fruit forest, their neighbour favours a sea of herbs. I like to think that we would display a touch of individualism, that our choices – and hence our garden – would reflect our personality, perhaps even be one of the ways in which we allow that self to develop. A garden will do that for you, if you let it.

If this book does one thing, I hope it will uncurl your fingers from familiar choices. Those familiars may be perfectly fantastic – ideal for you even – but let them alone for now: they're not going anywhere. You can always grasp them later if they're still the ones you want.

This book is also an invitation to ask yourself a few questions. Do you want to grow expensive food rather than cheap? Is flavour or yield more important to you? What is your favourite food? How much time do you want to commit? Are you open to the possibility that you might be embarking on something far more rewarding, far more happy-making, far more profoundly important even than eating delicious, nourishing meals?

Amongst the couple of hundred edible plants in these pages, there is everything from the ubiquitous to the unusual: none are inherently 'better' than others. To some, none of the plants in this book will be new: people have long grown even the most uncommon foods herein. Remember, there are no right answers: if you want to grow potatoes, then do; if loquats are your fancy, give them space. My only hope is that you grow something, and that you grow it in the way that gives you the most reward and pleasure.

Love what you have

Many people perceive themselves as being in transition: on the way to a new job, that house, more land, a perfect future. It rarely arrives, largely because we take ourselves with us. More often than not, any improvements we ask of life are more about ourselves than our lot – and so it is too with our gardens.

To be alive where you are is the key to happy gardening. Imagine you will live where you do for years (and often, that's exactly how it works out). Don't hesitate in planting an asparagus bed – the worst that will happen is that you move and leave something that will brighten the springtimes of those that follow for the next couple of decades. Scratch that: the worse that can happen is you don't plant if for fear of moving on, and three years later when you should be living off the tender green spears, you're still there umming and ahhing about whether to plant or not. This was me at our first house. Within a few weeks of moving to the second, out came the spade – I planted asparagus crown after asparagus crown. Don't waste the time I did in between. Live like this is the only place you'll ever garden. If it's too small to be your ideal garden, take the free time as an opportunity to enjoy something else; if it's too large, share it.

Limitations are often to do with attitude and perceived

ideals. Be positive. If your soil isn't ideal, you can improve it; if it's non-existent or truly awful, a raised bed or containers will overcome. While a sunny spot may allow you to grow the majority of plants that need plenty of warmth and light to produce well, there are leaves, sour cherries and currants amongst the many that find happiness in the shade. Detach yourself from the myth that summer harvests are necessarily more desirable or delicious than those from cooler months – celeriac is no less fabulous than a tomato, a fistful of sprouting broccoli is every bit as good as a pepper. There is always something delicious to grow whatever your patch – find yours and enjoy it.

Remember: there is almost always a way of growing something, whatever your space. Very dwarfing rootstocks can hold almonds and most other fruit and nuts to 1.5 metres in height and spread; blueberries will thrive in pots with ericaceous compost if your soil doesn't suit them; while a combination of rootstock and training can keep most fruit trees to a size that will flourish in a pot on a balcony. If there is a way, this book will show you it.

Lastly, love what you have because it might end up being exactly where and what you want it to be. The next place isn't always better; the larger piece of land not necessarily an incremental pleasure. If you ask for something else, you might find it's not what you thought it would be – you might realise you already had it.

Choosing what to grow

Choosing what to grow is really choosing what to eat. Almost. Let your tastebuds decide for you and allow your sense of anticipation to lead your decision making, then you are unlikely to be disappointed when it comes to the eating.

Take time to decide what you'll grow and ask yourself: do I want gluts, a steadier supply or a mix of both? Is saving money a priority? Am I looking for some new flavours and experiences from my garden? Would I like my garden to be beautiful?

All are important, yes, but keep at the front of your thoughts that flavour inspires pleasure – it should be your guide. A handful of something full of flavour will enrich your life and encourage you to grow more of it. A wheelbarrowful of mediocrity is enough to put anyone off.

Even if your primary aspiration is to provide yourself with the core of your meals, your kitchen garden – whatever form it takes – can be a place of pleasure and of eye-opening flavours, where life balance can (miraculously) be restored. Whether it's solitude, companionability, somewhere to share with loved ones, exercise or relaxation you are looking for, your kitchen garden can offer it in abundance.

Providing you bite off what you can chew and tailor your garden to your life, your kitchen garden should light up rather than weigh down your life. The trick, as in most things in life, is to find a starting point that suits you. This is essential. Many people overstretch and give up gardening quickly, often blaming the world for not telling them that growing food was so much work. There is no such thing. If I gave you a pot of mint to look after, I suspect even the busiest amongst you would find it hard not to dedicate yourself to the once-in-a-while watering it requires. The key is to start small and build up, rather than overstretch and work back.

One thing I hope to do is to convince you that the familiar flavours are not necessarily the ones you'll enjoy most. Most food in the supermarkets is there because its qualities suit the transport and storage necessary for it to reach the shelves in good visual condition, while resistance to disease is likely to have played more of a role in their selection than flavour. You can be confident that the French beans you buy are probably not that close to the finest they can be; and a mulberry or a wineberry are no less spectacular than a strawberry, despite their absence from the shelves.

Like everyone, I have favourites – flavours that I love or particularly connect with – and I will be unable to keep some preferences from becoming apparent. Feel free to ignore me or disagree when it occurs. Or take it as a challenge to try that hated brassica one more time, a different way to how you've had it before – it may just turn out to be special.

Despite giving equal prominence to less familiar foods, I remain enthusiastic of the well known. It is, after all, quite hard to improve upon the first new potatoes of the year or a handful of sunwarmed strawberries.

And lastly, I'm expecting – hoping even – that you'll disagree with me, that I might challenge or infuriate from time to time. All of that is crucial to getting to where you should be, with the kitchen garden that suits and works for you, and that provides you with fine food and pleasure in equal measure.

WHAT TO GROW

VEGETABLES

AGRETTI

Salsola soda. Also known as: European barilla plant, opposite-leaved saltwort, monk's beard and barba di frate. Hardy annual.

Agretti has been a real fixture in my garden in recent years. The slightly succulent texture and gentle mineral flavour of its slender leaves (like a green monk's beard, hence its name) go perfectly with eggs and fish and other seafood, and it adds delightful punctuation to almost any salad. Agretti has a wonderful texture and flavour raw, but is also happy to be cooked briefly - either steamed or sautéed. It's hard to find a finer lunch than an agretti tortilla.

VARIETIES: Generic.

STARTING OFF: Sow seed in late winter or early spring, as it needs cold to germinate. Sow in modules or direct into the ground 5–10mm deep. Germination can be erratic so sow twice as many seeds as you want plants.

POSITION: Full sun and light soil ideally – to suit its Mediterranean seaside origins.

SPACING: 20–30cm apart.

PRODUCTIVITY/EFFICIENCY: A great cut-and-come-again vegetable that's hard to find in the shops.

GROWING: Grows to full size (50cm height and 30cm spread) in less than two months. Each plant will grow into a small succulent bush that can be kept in shape with frequent harvesting. Easy to grow and pretty much pest free.

POTENTIAL PROBLEMS: Leaves can turn tough early in autumn. Seed is extremely short lived, with only a few months' viability.

HARVEST: Cut the green tops off the plants when they have reached 20cm – they will soon re-sprout and can be cut again.

ASPARAGUS

Asparagus officinalis. Hardy perennial.

In mid-spring, asparagus provides the vegetable equivalent of that first mouthful of cider on a summer's afternoon when you should be working - it virtually defines springtime. It is the embodiment of the uniqueness of home-grown flavour - eat the slim spears cooked within a few minutes of cutting and you'll understand what makes otherwise grumpy old men and cranky old women leap from their beds brandishing asparagus knives during April and May. As good as food gets.

Asparagus needs little cooking - just a few minutes' steaming or simmering in water is plenty - it should be just tender. Hollandaise, mayonnaise, butter, pepper and Parmesan all go beautifully with asparagus. Do try it raw too - it has a flavour very like bright, fresh, unsalted peanuts.

VARIETIES: 'Darlise' is a very fine, vigorous French variety. 'Stuarts Purple' is one of the few purple varieties to retain its colour on cooking – tasty and tender. 'Connover's Colossal' is an old variety – flavourful and chunky, perfect for a late-season harvest.

STARTING OFF: Although asparagus can be started from seed, I'd suggest planting crowns – dormant clumps of roots – in early spring. Dig a ditch to a spade's depth and within it create a ridge, then lay the crowns over it. Cover with soil and water well.

POSITION: Sunny and well drained.

SPACING: 40cm apart.

PRODUCTIVITY/EFFICIENCY: A little work planting, some patience while they establish, but then low maintenance for a couple of decades of delicious productivity.

GROWING: Asparagus hates competition, so keep the bed weed free. Cut the stems back almost to the ground when they turn yellow in autumn/early winter.

POTENTIAL PROBLEMS: Watch out for asparagus beetle on mature plants (pick them off by hand), and protect young plants from slug damage.

HARVEST: Pick your first few spears 2 years after planting. The following year, harvest for just 6 weeks then stop to allow the plants to build up reserves for the following year.

AUBERGINE

Solarium melongena. Frost-tender perennial.

I eat aubergines in more varied ways each year and, perhaps not by coincidence. I'm also getting better at growing them. Growing aubergines is a bit of a gamble: you need to kick them off early with heat and light and then hope that the bit you can't control - the summer - is sunny and long. If all the stars align, late summer will present you with really superb aubergines - likely smaller than those in the shops, but with such fine flavour and texture. They are at their best thinly sliced, lightly olive oiled and griddled. Their affinity for cumin (and, therefore, perilla) should be explored, especially in a curry.

VARIETIES: 'Moneymaker' and 'Slim Jim' are early and reliable varieties with taut, deep purple, shiny skins. They don't tend to grow too large, so are good for cool areas. You could also try the beautifully coloured 'Turkish Orange'. Perfect for a container, this Turkish heirloom variety produces small fruits that turn from green to orange, and have sweet flesh with little bitterness.

STARTING OFF: Aubergines need heat and light and a long growing season, so should be started off in February or March in modules or small pots in a heated propagator or airing cupboard. Once growing, pot on as the roots begin to show at the base until you reach a 30cm container. Either grow in the pot or plant into the ground in late May or June, ideally under cover. Consider young grafted plants: they are quick to mature and hence the fruit get more of the summer's heat.

POSITION: Full sun and shelter, in a well-draining soil or compost. Best in the warmth of a greenhouse or polytunnel.

SPACING: 60cm apart.

PRODUCTIVITY/EFFICIENCY: Rarely highly productive in Britain, but the flavour and texture of home-grown aubergines is very special. Plants need plenty of feeding and warmth.

GROWING: Feed with a comfrey or seaweed feed every fortnight as soon as your plants have flowered. When the plants reach 30cm tall, pinch out the growing tip to encourage side shoots, and be sure to stake your plants. For larger varieties of aubergine allow only 5 or 6 fruit to develop, removing all other flowers.

POTENTIAL PROBLEMS: Aubergines need really warm weather to perform well and may fail to produce fruits in cooler summers. Spraying with water to increase humidity should discourage red spider mites, but you can use a biological pest control *Phytoseiulus persimilis* if this doesn't work. Aphids can usually be rubbed off as they appear but also try companion planting with basil.

HARVEST: Cut fruits in late summer when they are firm and shiny.

BAMBOO

Various species - see below. Evergreen perennial.

Many years ago, when my couple of bamboos were getting established, Martin Crawford (author of *Creating A Forest Garden*) cooked me lunch of bamboo shoots, Good King Henry and sweet cicely seeds - it was my first taste of freshly harvested bamboo and it was incredible. Happily, mine are now throwing up plenty of crisp, fresh shoots every year - they seem to go through a door, before which they are slow, after which they are highly productive. Shoots can easily grow to 30cm in a couple of days, and should be picked no larger as they'll be tough. Their flavour isn't powerful, but rather like an interesting courgette. Non-bitter varieties can be eaten raw, or otherwise steamed for 10 minutes.

VARIETIES: There are many species of bamboo, all of which are edible. Generally speaking the Phyllostachys species are most productive in cooler climates like the UK. *Phyllostachys edulis* throws up shoots in spring whereas *P. aurea* produces them in autumn and both of which can be eaten raw. You could also try *P. viridiglaucescens* (early summer and also good raw) or *Pleioblastus simonii* (late summer, needs steaming to remove bitterness).

STARTING OFF: Source plants from a good supplier or divide established clumps.

POSITION: Tolerant of most moist soils and prefers light to moderate shade.

SPACING: This is dependent on species but running types such as Phyllostachys are keen to spread by throwing up new shoots, sometimes many feet away. Happily, once cut the shoots don't regrow and in this way the plant is easily kept within your chosen area.

PRODUCTIVITY/EFFICIENCY: Bamboos are very productive. With careful choice of varieties you can have young shoots from spring to autumn and with each variety producing new shoots over a period of 2–3 months. Some varieties like *Phyllostachys dulcis* begin putting up shoots in early spring when little else is around to eat.

GROWING: Little maintenance required. If harvested regularly then an annual mulch of compost will be needed or grow a nitrogen-fixing tree or shrub nearby.

POTENTIAL PROBLEMS: Control spread by cutting young shoots.

HARVEST: From spring to autumn, cut shoots at ground level, or just below, when it is around 30cm long. Remove the outer layers until you reach the tender pale green to white flesh.

BEETROOT

Beta vulgaris. Hardy biennial.

I'm genuinely mystified as to the divide between beetroot lovers and haters – this is one of the must-haves of my garden. Reliable, easy, provider of delicious sweet roots and really under-appreciated leaves – I can only put any dislike down to poorly pickled beets eaten in childhood. Sow a few rows of the varieties below in spring and see if you still dislike them by early summer when they're harvested. Washed, unpeeled and roasted beetroots become deliciously sweet and earthy with rosemary, garlic and a little oil.

VARIETIES: 'Barbietola di Chioggia', with its glorious concentric candy stripes, and 'Burpees Golden', with its deep ginger flesh, are as beautiful as they are delicious. Essentials. For large, sweet, tender roots of classic deep rich purple, try 'Sanguina' or 'Bolivar'.

STARTING OFF: Sow 2 or 3 seeds on to each module in March, thinning to the strongest couple when they've germinated, planting them out in April, under fleece if you like. Subsequent sowings can be made direct every few weeks for a good supply throughout the summer and autumn months.

POSITION: Full sun is best, though will take a little shade. Well-composted ground is ideal.

SPACING: Thin to 7cm apart, or further apart if you prefer bigger beetroots.

PRODUCTIVITY/EFFICIENCY: Easy and cheap, needing little care as they grow.

GROWING: Water through extended dry periods.

POTENTIAL PROBLEMS: Generally trouble free, though snails and slugs can make small holes later in the season and birds can occasionally bother the seedlings.

HARVEST: Harvest the largest bulbs in each row by gripping the stems and pulling gently. The bulbs should come up easily. Any neighbours left behind will swell to fill the space. For baby beetroot harvest from 7 weeks after sowing. Seedlings thinned out can be added to salads.

BORLOTTI BEAN

Phaseolus vulgaris. Frost-tender annual.

I wouldn't grow many things just for looks - that'd be crossing over to the dark side where ornamental gardeners live - but for borlottis I'd make a rare exception. Lively climbing beans that skate up their support in search of light and heat, hanging glorious red and cream speckled pods as soon as they can. The beans within are one of my favourites - nutty, creamy and flavourful in themselves yet happy to take on strong flavours like garlic, chilli and the woody herbs. Great used fresh and store well into and out of winter for hearty soups and stews. A must.

VARIETIES: 'Lingua di Fuoco' is the most common variety – available also as a dwarf, which is good for exposed sites. You can occasionally find 'Lamon' – large and tasty beans, and the traditional variety for pasta e fagioli.

STARTING OFF: Sow from March until midsummer for beans from summer to autumn. Sow into root trainers under cover, then plant out from mid-May on to a sturdy framework of canes. Sow direct from late April until mid-July if you prefer.

POSITION: Full sun and a light, well-composted soil.

SPACING: 20cm apart.

PRODUCTIVITY/EFFICIENCY: Borlottis take up little floor space but grow tall, so are good for those looking to get a good harvest from limited garden room.

GROWING: Tie young plants into canes to help them on their way. A liquid or manure feed will boost the size of your crops, especially if grown in a container. Save some of your crop for sowing the following year.

POTENTIAL PROBLEMS: Slugs can be troublesome when the plants are young.

HARVEST: Harvest beans in late summer into autumn to eat fresh while the pods are plump with beans, either when the beans are green or leave them on the plant and harvest when the plants are beginning to desiccate. You can use the beans demi-sec like this, or cut the plant at the base and hang it upside down to dry the beans for a few days more.

BROAD BEAN

Vicia faba. Hardy annual.

Worth growing just for the scent of the flowers - as happy-making as any ornamental - and the leafy tops which grow above the pods. Sliced off and stir fried they are one of the great unbuyable gardener's treats. The beans themselves are equally special, particularly if picked small - they are sweet and less bitter than when allowed to plump up. Equally importantly, picking them early encourages the plant to produce more, so you get no less in the way of yield.

VARIETIES: 'Bunyard's Exhibition' is my favourite with its reliably delicious, tender beans. For autumn sowing, 'Aquadulce Claudia' is a tough, hardy variety that grows slowly through winter to give early spring beans. 'The Sutton' is a dwarf that's ideal for windy spots or containers, but whatever your situation, make a little space for the beautiful 'Crimson Flowered'.

STARTING OFF: Sow hardy types 5cm deep straight into the ground in autumn, or into root trainers under cover in late winter, planting out from March onwards. In spring you can sow direct too but I tend to start most of mine under cover to get them off to a good start out of the way of the slugs.

POSITION: Sunny, well drained and ideally sheltered.

SPACING: 20cm apart, with 60cm between rows.

PRODUCTIVITY/EFFICIENCY: A spring sowing will be ready to harvest in around 3 months. The secret with broad beans is to sow in repeated small batches every 2 weeks or so, to avoid gluts and give you a steady harvest. The legume family (of which beans are part) enrich the soil by capturing nitrogen from the air and making it available in the soil – cut the plant at the base when the beans are harvested, to improve fertility for the plants that follow.

GROWING: Sow every fortnight or so through spring and early summer for a steady harvest, with plants ready to replace those that tire. Broad beans are tall plants and may need support. Push canes into the ground at the ends of the rows and tie string between them. Pinching out the growing tips when the first tiny pods are beginning to appear will direct the plant's energy to the developing pods.

POTENTIAL PROBLEMS: Plants sown in autumn can weather badly, so cover with fleece or with a cloche if possible. Black aphids love broad beans – wipe them off with a cloth when you see them; pinching out the tips helps.

HARVEST: Spring-sown beans will be ready in three months or so, with autumn-sown beans ready to pick in mid-spring.

BRUSSELS SPROUTS

Brassica oleracea var. *gemmifera.* Hardy biennial.

One of my favourite winter vegetables, but I confess to growing only a small proportion of my consumption. Much as I love them - for the mini cabbages that sit on top of their trunk as much as the sprouts themselves - they are in the ground for an awfully long time (getting on for a year for later varieties). Much as they deliver in flavour, they take up a vast amount of space. A couple of lines, happily taken for tops and sprouts, are all I afford them - the rest I buy.

If you are a non-believer, try them thinly sliced and fried in olive oil with bacon, with thyme and cream, or in place of the cabbage in coleslaw. The tops are as fine tasting as any brassica - slice, steam and serve with lemon juice and olive oil.

VARIETIES: 'Noisette' is a particularly nutty early season variety for sprouts from October to Christmas. Traditional late varieties like 'Seven Hills' or 'Wellington' will give you sprouts when little else is around. You could also try 'Red Rubine' and 'Red Bull' for lovely purple and red sprouts.

STARTING OFF: Sprouts need a long growing season. Start them under cover in modules in early spring, potting on as needed and planting out from mid-May to June when around 10–15cm tall. Don't allow the plant's growth to be checked by delaying potting on. Firm them in well.

POSITION: Sunny position. Sprouts will do well in heavy soils. Preferably mildly alkaline soil, but not essential.

SPACING: 60cm apart.

PRODUCTIVITY/EFFICIENCY: Sprouts need little maintenance and certain varieties can crop over a long period of time. Sow salad leaves, radishes or herbs around newly planted sprouts to make good use of space, or nasturtiums to cover the ground quickly, while retaining water and providing a harvest.

GROWING: Sprouts are tall but shallow rooting, so tread the soil down firmly when planting out and, if exposed, use a cane for support.

POTENTIAL PROBLEMS: Cabbage white butterflies and caterpillars can cause huge damage on unprotected crops. Plant nasturtiums as a sacrificial crop and/or use canes to create a cage of fleece or similar to exclude them completely – place it over the plants as soon as they are planted out.

HARVEST: If you want your sprouts to mature all at once, chop the top off the plant in October (or choose a cultivar that naturally matures its sprouts together), otherwise, snap the sprouts off using a downward action when they reach a suitable size.

BUCK'S HORN PLANTAIN

Plantago coronopus. Also known as: minutina, plantago and erba stella. Hardy perennial often grown as an annual.

This is a succulent salad leaf, sweeter and nuttier than spinach and with a faint hint of parsley. Harvest the leaves young and before the plant begins to flower, when they are at their most tender. Don't miss out on the flowers though as they are also great in salads. A native of coastal areas in Europe, it thrives in cool, rainy conditions, and also won't mind saline soil.

VARIETIES: Generic.

STARTING OFF: The seed is tiny so sow in trays under cover from February, prick out into modules and plant out when roots are showing. You can also sow direct in early spring.

POSITION: Most soils with good drainage. Sun or light shade.

SPACING: 20cm apart.

PRODUCTIVITY/EFFICIENCY: A small patch can provide you with leaves for salads or for steaming from April to June (longer if you cut back flower stems).

GROWING: Cut back flower stems to promote fresh leaf growth.

POTENTIAL PROBLEMS: Generally pest and disease free.

HARVEST: Pick young leaves while tender and before the plants flower. Leaves can be eaten fresh or lightly steamed.

CABBAGE

Brassica oleracea var. *capitata*. Hardy biennial.

I don't grow many cabbages, but I always, always have a line or two of 'January King'. It looks and tastes fabulous and the texture has the sort of stature you expect in a robust kale - making it perfectly happy to stand next to chilli, olive oil and garlic. Other than that, do consider a few spring cabbages - they may look tatty once they've hauled themselves out of winter, but beneath the outer leaves they're an early season smasher when there's little else around.

VARIETIES: With the right varieties you can be harvesting cabbage all year round. Try spring varieties 'Myatt's Offenham' or 'Pixie'. For summer cabbages I grow 'Hispi', 'Greyhound' or 'Marner Early Red'. Good autumn/winter varieties to try are 'Cuor di Bue', 'January King' and 'Best of All'.

STARTING OFF: Sow cabbages in modules under cover. Summer and autumn cabbages should be sown in March, winter cabbages in May, and spring cabbages in July/August. Plant out under fleece or Enviromesh 6 weeks later. Pot on and plant out when around 8–10cm tall. Cabbages, as with all brassicas, don't like their roots being checked, so plant out as soon as the roots are showing through the holes in the bottom of the pot.

POSITION: Full sun. Will do well in heavy ground.

SPACING: 25–50cm apart, depending on variety.

PRODUCTIVITY/EFFICIENCY: Cabbages will occupy space in your veg patch for around 16 weeks but without requiring much input from you. Make use of the space between your cabbages early on in summer and autumn by direct sowing leafy salad crops like summer purslane or herbs.

GROWING: Water in and firm the soil down well when planting. Water during dry spells to keep growth good and steady.

POTENTIAL PROBLEMS: Protect from cabbage white butterflies and caterpillars, and pigeons, with fleece or take your chances. Slugs can also do plenty of damage, so hunt out and pick off frequently. Clubroot can build up if brassicas are grown for too long in the same patch of ground, so don't grow them for consecutive years in one spot. Adding lime to the soil to increase its relative alkalinity can help rectify clubroot.

HARVEST: Use a sharp knife to cut the whole head once a firm heart has formed.

CALABRESE

Brassica oleracea var. *Italica*. Hardy biennial.

Another of my favourite vegetables (usually sold as 'broccoli' in the shops). It's quicker from sowing to harvest than many brassicas, but frustratingly I don't grow them well. Don't let that put you off - they aren't tricky; I just don't have the knack, but I am trying again this year after a couple of years off as I love calabrese steamed or broken into florets and roasted with lemon and olive oil.

VARIETIES: 'Chevalier' is reliable and has a good flavour. 'Green Comet' is good for early crops.

STARTING OFF: Calabrese is prone to bolting at any perceived slight, and won't take well to transplanting. Sow short rows direct into the ground from April to early summer, or sow in modules under cover from March until June and take care not to disturb the roots when planting out. You can also sow in October under cover for a spring polytunnel crop.

POSITION: Full sun in a well-drained and composted soil is ideal, though it can take some shade.

SPACING: 25–30cm apart.

PRODUCTIVITY/EFFICIENCY: You will have your first crops of calabrese 3–4 months after sowing, with little maintenance required.

GROWING: Steady growth is important, so prevent plants from drying out in hot weather.

POTENTIAL PROBLEMS: As with all brassicas, cabbage white butterfly, pigeons and clubroot are the main things to look out for. Try planting nasturtiums nearby to attract the butterflies or fleece against them (and the pigeons). Lime if clubroot is a problem and don't grow brassicas in the same place 2 years in a row. Soil must be kept moist or the threat of bolting rears its head again.

HARVEST: Harvest when they are firm and before any of the buds have started to turn to flowers. You should find smaller side shoots appear providing you with a second crop.

CALLALOO

Amaranthus species. Half-hardy annual.

A delicious and beautifully ornamental plant, with leaves that taste somewhere between spinach and watercress. Hugely popular in West Indian cooking, this easy, fast-growing, impressive plant produces leaves that can be coloured anywhere from green through to vibrant red. If allowed, it will grow tall and produce wonderful seed heads in late summer. Use the leaves as you would spinach.

VARIETIES: Callaloo seed is usually sold under the generic name common amaranth. You could try varieties 'Hopi Red Leaf' or 'Callaloo', which do well in cooler areas.

STARTING OFF: Sow seed in modules under cover in April. Pot on if necessary before planting out after the last frosts.

POSITION: Full sun and good drainage.

SPACING: Around 45cm apart.

PRODUCTIVITY/EFFICIENCY: Callaloo is a vigorous plant, taking up reasonable space but providing you with greens for several months from June. The seeds are also edible. Covers the ground well and is grown as a block, so needs little weeding or watering.

GROWING: Keep picking the shoots to prevent the plants from flowering and to encourage more shoots to form.

POTENTIAL PROBLEMS: Generally pest and disease free.

HARVEST: Pick leaves and shoots for steaming once plants are well established – usually from June until September.

CARDOON

Cynara cardunculus. Hardy perennial.

Growing to 3m at times, and almost indistinguishable in appearance from globe artichokes, cardoons give structure and year-round presence to a garden. I love them most in winter when they stand strong against the cold, wind and rain. The leaf stalks (looking like bodybuilder celery) can be stripped from the leafier part and steamed to eat as a crudité with dips or steamed before making into a gratin.

VARIETIES: Cardoons are generally sold as unnamed varieties, but if you can find them try 'Argente de Geneve' or 'Gigante di Romagna'.

STARTING OFF: Buy as small plants or start seed in early spring in modules under cover.

POSITION: Tolerant of poor soils and grow well in shade, but happiest in full sun.

SPACING: 80cm apart.

PRODUCTIVITY/EFFICIENCY: Whilst cardoons do take up a large amount of space there is little work to do with them and the flowers are marvellous for the bees.

GROWING: Leave dead flowers and flower stems on the plant over winter and cut back hard in spring as the new leaves start to shoot. After a few years of growth, split clumps of cardoons in autumn and replant or pot up.

POTENTIAL PROBLEMS: Slugs can attack young plants, but beyond this vulnerable stage cardoons are trouble free.

HARVEST: The edible part of cardoons is their celery-like stems. On a dry day in late summer, gather together the leaves, wrap a collar of card or thick newspaper around them, tie it in place and leave for around 4 weeks to blanch.

CARROTS

Daucus carota. Hardy biennial.

To my mind, there are two types of carrot: early, expensive to buy, occupy their space for a short time, sweet and small; and large, late, relatively cheap and perfectly fine carrots. I grow only the first, for reasons that I hope are obvious. Many of the earlies are eaten straight from the ground, soil brushed off and leafy tops cast semi-accurately at the compost bin. Lifted early, they free up space for another batch or a different crop.

VARIETIES: With a polytunnel, the right varieties and storage you can have carrots for a good part of the year. Try 'Nantes' and 'Chantenay' for a classic sweet and early carrot. 'Paris Market' is another early sweet variety – it comes golf-ball sized and shaped and is good for a heavier soil. Late winter storing varieties are 'Autumn King' and 'Flakee'. 'Rainbow Mix' is an early maincrop, which includes white, yellow and purple varieties.

STARTING OFF: Best sown direct. Early varieties can be sown successively from March to June outside for a good supply of small sweet roots throughout the summer, and from February to August if growing in a tunnel. Sow carrots for storage in May or June.

POSITION: Full sun in a well-drained and stone-free soil. Compost/manure isn't needed.

SPACING: Sow seed thinly in shallow drills 15cm apart or broadcast sparsely and rake in. Thin to around 7cm.

PRODUCTIVITY/EFFICIENCY: A small piece of ground can yield good crops of carrots over a long period of time.

GROWING: Keep weeded and well watered.

POTENTIAL PROBLEMS: Carrot fly is the main nuisance. Use fleece or companion plant with something oniony.

HARVEST: Pull early carrots as soon as they are ready from May onwards. You can leave maincrops to overwinter in the ground, but if rain or severe cold is threatening they can be dug up and stored (unwashed) in paper sacks or in crates or boxes with slightly damp sand.

CAULIFLOWER

Brassica oleracea var. *botrytis*. Hardy biennial.

I can't seem to not grow cauliflower, no matter how hard I try. I love them but they take an age to mature and, tediously, they will 'blow' with almost no provocation - turning from tight, pat-able heads into floating florets, losing much of their crisp texture in the process. But still, against my better nature, I continue to grow a few each year - usually a line split between coloured varieties and 'All The Year Round'. More often than not, I break them into florets and roast them after marinating in spicy yoghurt.

VARIETIES: It is possible to have cauliflowers throughout the year with careful choice of variety. In grave infringement of the Trades Descriptions Act, 'All The Year Round' will give you cauliflowers from June to October. 'Purple Cape' is ready in March/April and 'Aalsmeer' in April/May when there's not much else around. Whatever time of year you are looking to harvest, there will be mini varieties, such as 'Igloo', to suit.

STARTING OFF: Sow when variety requires, starting in modules. Pot on into 9cm pots and plant out when 7–10cm tall.

POSITION: Full sun in a sheltered site on a moisture-retentive, well-manured/composted soil.

SPACING: 45–70cm apart for large cauliflowers, depending on variety, and 15cm for mini ones.

PRODUCTIVITY/EFFICIENCY: Winter cauliflowers in particular take up a lot of space (approx. 70cm) and for around 40 weeks of the year. Summer and autumn varieties will be in the ground for around 16 weeks.

GROWING: Cauliflowers do not like any check to their growth so ensure they are planted out in good time with the soil firmed thoroughly around them, and watered well in dry weather. To keep heads protected against the worst of the weather, bend a few of the outer leaves over them by snapping the central rib.

POTENTIAL PROBLEMS: Fleece against pigeons and butterflies. Lime the soil if clubroot is a problem.

HARVEST: Cut the stalk below the head when the cauliflower has a nicely formed globe, and before it gets the chance to bolt (most likely in hot weather).

CELERIAC

Apium graveolens var. *rapaceum.* Hardy biennial.

A fine, rough and wrinkled ball of savoury earthiness that's one of winter's staple harvests for me. Its flavour is nominally of a potato crossed with celery, but far lovelier than that implies – there's an easy sweetness that sets off any gentle bitterness.

If you're not too worried about producing prize specimens, it's fairly easy to get a good crop, but for the plumpest, large celeriac they'll need sun and moisture and not to be held up in modules when they're ready to plant out

Peel and either chop or slice celeriac depending on the recipe and submerge into acidulated water to prevent discolouring. It makes perhaps an even finer dauphinoise than the traditional potato version, and is superb in coleslaw – combine equal quantities of matchstick-sized celeriac, carrot and apple in a mustardy dressing.

VARIETIES: I can't tell varieties apart for flavour, but 'Prinz' and 'Tellus' are both reliable.

STARTING OFF: In February/early March sow seed in modules in a tunnel or greenhouse and plant into final position as the soil warms up. The seeds are very small so sow as few as possible in each module and thin to one seedling.

POSITION: Full sun and tolerant of light shade. Keep soil moist in dry weather.

SPACING: 40cm apart.

PRODUCTIVITY/EFFICIENCY: Celeriac is pretty low maintenance but takes up space for a good part of the year.

GROWING: As the roots swell, remove the lower leaf stalks around the base to encourage larger roots.

POTENTIAL PROBLEMS: Largely disease free but slugs do appreciate them.

HARVEST: Except in the coldest of weather, celeriac can remain in the ground until March, digging as needed. If the celeriac is dug up for storage then remove the leaves for longevity. Once established, take a few leaves to use in place of lovage, adding savoury stock flavours to stews and soups.

CELERY

Apium graveolens var. *dulce.* Hardy biennial.

The single vegetable that I can't bear to eat raw; even worse, paired with the cavity wall insulation that is cottage cheese. As a flavouring I love its slim ridged stalks – in soup and stews especially, its savouriness is a must, though I am as likely to get it from the leaves of lovage or celeriac which are very similar in taste. Grow the self-blanching varieties for ease.

VARIETIES: Older varieties such as 'Solid Pink' require blanching in a trench but many of the newer ones – such as 'Green Utah' and 'Golden Self-Blanching' – do it themselves, taking much of the grief away. The older varieties tend to be hardier with a more delicate flavour.

STARTING OFF: In March/early April, sow seed into modules under cover and plant into their final position as the soil warms up. The seeds are very small so sow as few as possible in each module and thin to one seedling.

POSITION: Tolerates some shade and needs a fertile moisture-retentive soil with good drainage.

SPACING: Self-blanching types are best planted in a block with 15–30cm between plants. Celery that requires blanching should be planted 30–45cm apart in the trench with 1.5m between trenches.

PRODUCTIVITY/EFFICIENCY: Self-blanching types will be in the ground for up to 16 weeks and trench celery for 9 months.

GROWING: Keep weed free and water well in dry spells.

POTENTIAL PROBLEMS: Starting in modules minimises slug and snail damage. Planting out in May should reduce the risk of celery fly damage.

HARVEST: Self-blanching celery can be harvested when it reaches the desired size, from July until the first frosts.

CHARD AND PERPETUAL SPINACH

Beta vulgaris var. *flavescens*. Hardy biennial.

Almost unnoticed, chard (and to a degree perpetual spinach) has edged its way on to my never-without list. As lazily productive as any vegetable I can think of, these glorious leaves can be harvested throughout the year. Once you get to know them, you'll appreciate their easy reliability, flavour and the generosity of crisp stalks and robust, yet not in any way tough, leaves. I'd not want to be without them.

VARIETIES: 'White Silver' for large and delicious leaves and a thick rib, 'Bright Lights' for smaller leaves with ribs ranging from yellows through oranges to red. 'Canary Yellow' and 'Lucullus' are some of the best for baby salad leaves.

STARTING OFF: Sow in modules in March/April and again in July, planting out when 3–4cm tall.

POSITION: Largely unfussy, and will tolerate some shade and a coastal spot.

SPACING: 10–15cm apart for baby leaves, 30cm between smaller varieties like 'Bright Lights' and 45cm for the largest.

PRODUCTIVITY/EFFICIENCY: From only two sowings you can have year-round cut-and-come-again leaves.

GROWING: Apart from watering in dry weather and keeping free of weeds, little else is required

POTENTIAL PROBLEMS: Slugs can make their mark on young plants and to a lesser degree in mature plants, but generally trouble free otherwise.

HARVEST: Cut leaves 5cm above the ground and the leaves will regrow.

CHERVIL AND PARSLEY ROOT

Chaerophyllum bulbosum and *Petroselinum crispum tuberosum*. Hardy biennial.

These two really should have their own entry but I've put them together because I ate them for the first time on the same day, and because broadly you treat them the same. Limp, I know. Do, please, grow both. These relatively uncommon roots are delicious - chervil root has a sweet, chestnutty earthiness, whereas parsley root (aka Hamburg parsley) has just a hint of parsley about it. Try both roasted in olive oil or made into crisps.

VARIETIES: No named varieties.

STARTING OFF: Chervil root needs around 8 weeks of cold to germinate (stratification) so either sow direct in autumn or mix with damp sand and store in the fridge for 8 weeks before sowing in March. Parsley root can be sown direct in March.

POSITION: Sunny site, in composted soil.

SPACING: 10cm apart with 30cm between rows, or in blocks with plants 20cm apart in all directions.

PRODUCTIVITY/EFFICIENCY: As with most roots, chervil root and parsley root will spend at least 8 months in the soil before you can harvest, but being relatively small, they needn't take up a lot of room. Low maintenance.

GROWING: Water during dry weather and keep weed free.

POTENTIAL PROBLEMS: Usually trouble free.

HARVEST: From September through January. Their flavour will improve after a frost.

CHICORY

Cichorium intybus. Hardy perennial usually grown as an annual.

Embrace the bitter! So many of us are in search for the sweet that we often lose all appreciation of how wonderful a nip of bitterness can be. Try chicory leaves sparingly in mixed leaf salads or, even better, as heads cut in half lengthways and fried in a little oil, adding a dash of vinegar and then double cream at the end – you'll be turned. There are many great varieties for growing too – some long, pale and slender, others round and vivid.

VARIETIES: Many, and varied in their habits too. Some chicories are hearting like 'Sugar Loaf' and 'Palla Rosa'; some are loose-leaved such as 'Catalogna Frastagliata'. There are puntarelle types with finger-like growth, as well as cut-and-come-again varieties, such as 'Italian Dandelion'. Others like 'Witloof' can be 'forced' for use over the coldest winter months.

STARTING OFF: Sow from March through to August depending on variety.

POSITION: Chicory will do well in most soils except the lightest and heaviest. It will tolerate some shade.

SPACING: 20–30cm apart depending on variety.

PRODUCTIVITY/EFFICIENCY: Chicories can be in the ground for many months but much of it can be over the winter, when there is less demand on space. Takes well to pick and come again. They can supply you with greens in early spring when little else is around.

GROWING: Once established, chicory is very drought tolerant. May need protection over the coldest months.

POTENTIAL PROBLEMS: Usually trouble free.

HARVEST: Harvest leaves individually through the coldest months from loose-leaved varieties. Hearting varieties may re-sprout from the stump after cutting.

CHILLI PEPPERS

Capsicum annuum. Frost-tender perennial, usually grown as an annual.

Chillies are the quintessential transformers, enlivening everything they come into contact with. With the right choice of varieties, chillies can give you everything from heart-stopping heat to gentle fruitiness, far beyond the narrow range of most shop-bought chillies. All take to pickling and freezing as well as being very good stored in olive oil. I like to grow a few varieties at once, so I have different flavours and strengths to choose from.

VARIETIES: Many and varied ranging from mild to extraordinarily hot. Try 'Apricot', 'Padron' or 'Poblano' for something mild and fruity, a mid-heat 'Bulgarian Carrot' or 'Bird's Eye', or 'Scotch Bonnet' for something truly hot. Don't demonstrate your diminutive sexual organs by trying 'Dorset Naga' – at over 1 million on the Scoville scale of chilli heat, they are hundreds of times hotter than most you buy.

STARTING OFF: In modules in a propagator or airing cupboard in February/March, potting on into 9cm pots and then again as soon as the roots show through the holes in the bottom. Generally speaking, it should be warm enough to plant in a tunnel or greenhouse by the end of April. Germination is usually slow.

POSITION: As hot, sunny and sheltered as you can give them, ideally a tunnel or greenhouse.

C

SPACING: 45–60cm apart.

PRODUCTIVITY/EFFICIENCY: Chillies are particular early on, needing care and to be started early with heat. Once growing and with the occasional feed, chillies can be hugely productive and carry much flavour in a small parcel.

GROWING: Whilst in pots, feed with liquid comfrey or seaweed every week or so.

POTENTIAL PROBLEMS: Fairly trouble free, though watch for aphids and deal with them in whichever way you prefer. I like biological controls, such as ladybirds.

HARVEST: Depending on the summer, chillies are usually ready in September. Use them freshly picked or dry your excess on the lowest setting in your oven overnight.

CHINESE ARTICHOKE

Stachys affinis. Hardy perennial.

Popular in France where they are known as crosnes, Chinese artichokes resemble cream-coloured, segmented oca. Excellent raw in salads, lightly stir-fried or steamed, they have a nutty flavour and a pleasing water chestnut-like texture. An easy, delicious, unbuyable, underground treasure.

VARIETIES: No named varieties available.

STARTING OFF: Source tubers from a good supplier.

POSITION: Chinese artichokes are most productive in humus-rich, fertile soils. Tolerant of light shade.

SPACING: Chinese artichokes have a spreading habit, forming clumps, and are best planted 12cm or so apart and around 10cm deep.

PRODUCTIVITY/EFFICIENCY: Plentiful small tubers are produced with little effort on your part. Just re-plant some of the tubers to grow again next year.

GROWING: Little maintenance required except to keep them relatively weed free early in the year, and an annual mulch of compost.

POTENTIAL PROBLEMS: Generally pest and disease free.

HARVEST: Ready to harvest from late October, the tubers store happily in the soil over winter and can be dug as required.

CHINESE CEDAR

Toona sinensis. Deciduous tree/shrub.

Chinese cedar is one of the tastiest of the tree leaves, and hugely popular as a vegetable in China. The flavour is somewhere between garlic and onions - superb in stir-fries and salads. The leaves can be dried too (lay them in the sun in a greenhouse or polytunnel for a few days) and used as a spice.

VARIETIES: There are some named varieties but these have been bred for their ornamental qualities.

STARTING OFF: Can be started from seed but is unreliable. Best to source plants from a specialist supplier.

POSITION: A sunny spot and a moist but well-drained soil.

SPACING: A full-grown tree can reach 15m tall by 10m wide, but can easily be kept to 1–2m apart by coppicing and harvesting the shoots.

PRODUCTIVITY/EFFICIENCY: Once established, Chinese cedar will provide you with edible shoots with little work on your part, and can be underplanted with other edibles, as is common in Asia.

GROWING: Control its size by harvesting the young shoots and by coppicing occasionally.

POTENTIAL PROBLEMS: Generally pest and disease free.

HARVEST: Pick the young shoots before they exceed 20cm long, in spring and summer.

CHOP SUEY GREENS

Chrysanthemum coronarium. Also known as: *shungiku*. Hardy annual.

A peculiar thing, an edible chrysanthemum. The leaves and large daisy-like flowers have a distinctive, slightly aniseed flavour, best used in smallish amounts. Try young leaves and flowers in salads or more substantial leaves in stir-fries. Beautiful, too, bringing in beneficial insects as it flowers.

VARIETIES: No named varieties available.

STARTING OFF: Broadcast or sow in shallow drills from spring to September. Sow every few weeks for a good succession.

POSITION: Very happy in sun or part-shade.

SPACING: Thin to at least 5cm apart.

PRODUCTIVITY/EFFICIENCY: Harvesting is possible around 6 weeks after sowing and several cuttings can be had from each sowing.

GROWING: Water in dry weather.

POTENTIAL PROBLEMS: Fairly untroubled by pests and diseases but can become bitter in hot weather.

HARVEST: Cut when around 10cm high. The flowers are also edible.

CIME DI RAPA

Brassica rapa subsp. *rapa*. Also known as: broccolini, rapini, broccoli raab, broccoli rabe. Hardy annual.

Cime di rapa is essentially turnip tops, where the plant has been bred to produce more leaves and no root. Deliciously green and brassica-y in flavour, and takes very happily to cut-and-come-again harvesting. Try chopped and sautéed in olive oil, with garlic and lemon juice.

VARIETIES: No named varieties available.

STARTING OFF: Sow in modules in March, planting out in April. Sow again after midsummer through to September.

POSITION: Full sun, in a well-composted soil.

SPACING: 30cm apart.

PRODUCTIVITY/EFFICIENCY: Cime di rapa is ready to harvest in around 60 days and can regrow several times.

GROWING: Water through dry periods.

POTENTIAL PROBLEMS: Fleece plants if flea beetle is a problem.

HARVEST: Leaves, stalks, flower buds and flowers are all edible. Cut 5cm from the ground as required and your plants should re-sprout.

COURGETTES

Cucurbita pepo. Half-hardy annual.

Delicious, crisp cigars or hefty green water bags: the choice is yours. Harvest courgettes young and small to catch them at their best and the plant will quickly produce more for you. Thinly sliced, simply dressed and raw, they are a delight, as they are griddled. Make the most of the flowers too - peppery, with a crisp core, they are really good in salads, or stuffed, battered and deep-fried.

VARIETIES: 'Nero di Milano' and 'Tromboncino' are old varieties with the latter being vigorous and scrambling and producing swan-necked pale fruits. 'Romanesco' are ridged with huge flowers. 'Soleil' courgettes are yellow, 'Bianca di Trieste' are white and 'Rondo di Nizza' will give you round courgettes.

STARTING OFF: Sow seed individually in 9cm pots in April and plant out after the last frosts. Always sow two seeds plus one for each person you are growing for. If there are two of you, that's four plants: one for the slugs, and three (ideally of different varieties) to keep you in delicious small courgettes.

POSITION: Full sun in fertile, moisture-retentive soil.

SPACING: 90cm apart.

PRODUCTIVITY/EFFICIENCY: Plants can crop from June until early October, each plant producing many courgettes.

GROWING: Courgettes need a lot of water to produce well so ensure a good supply especially in dry weather.

POTENTIAL PROBLEMS: Slugs like young plants so take whichever measures you favour to deal with them. Cucumber mosaic virus is largely untreatable. Powdery mildew is a potential threat late in the season, so ensure good ventilation.

HARVEST: Plants give you a harvest of both flowers and courgettes. Look for the male flowers (those without a courgette forming behind the flower) – picking them won't reduce your courgette harvest. Pick courgettes when small for best flavour and keep picking to ensure a good supply.

CUCAMELONS

Melothria scabra. Tender perennial often grown as an annual.

A neighbour grew cucamelons a decade or so ago and we were relatively unimpressed, but we both gave them another try the following year and picked them a little earlier and they were much better - the first time, I suspect they'd gone a little past their best. Picked ripe yet crisp, as grape-sized mini-melons, their lightly citrus-cucumber flavour and texture is really good in salsas, salads and cocktails.

VARIETIES: No named varieties available.

STARTING OFF: Sow direct in April or in modules, potting on before planting out after the last frosts.

POSITION: Full sun and in moist but well-drained soil.

SPACING: Around 40cm apart.

PRODUCTIVITY/EFFICIENCY: Many small fruits are produced on each plant and over a long period of time. Cropping starts 9–12 weeks after sowing. Easy, relatively drought resistant and largely ignored by pests.

GROWING: Pinch out the growing tip when it reaches 2m or so,

C

and then pinch out any laterals when they reach 40cm. Provide support for the plants to climb up.

POTENTIAL PROBLEMS: Generally pest and disease free.

HARVEST: Pick cucamelons as they ripen from July to September.

CUCUMBERS AND GHERKINS

Cucumis sativus. Half-hardy annual.

I'm very fond of the few cucumbers I grow, especially the very beautiful 'Crystal Lemon' – ovate, yellow and it seems to be cooler than the green varieties and without any hint of bitterness in the skin. Cucumbers are not easy to coax a decent harvest from, but along with gherkins they have a flavour very much more satisfying than those you buy. I use most raw in salads, but increasingly in cocktails and for ice cream – both are as refreshing as they sound.

VARIETIES: 'Marketmore' for tasty cucumbers with good disease resistance; 'Crystal Lemon' has cool, crisp yellow fruit. 'La Diva' and 'Vert Petit de Paris' are small gherkins and good for pickling. 'Burpless Tendergreen' is a good ridge variety.

STARTING OFF: Start in 9cm pots under cover in April. Cucumbers can be planted outside after the last frosts.

POSITION: Full sun in a sheltered spot. Well-composted, moisture-retentive soil.

SPACING: 50cm apart for climbers and around 1.5m for ridge types to sprawl.

PRODUCTIVITY/EFFICIENCY: Cucumbers will produce from June until October if grown under cover.

GROWING: Cucumbers need a lot of water to produce well so ensure a good supply in dry weather.

POTENTIAL PROBLEMS: Red spider mite (treatable with the introduction of a natural predator, such as *Phytoseiulus persimilis*), cucumber mosaic virus (which is untreatable), and powdery mildew, which can be minimised with good ventilation.

HARVEST: Pick when a good size but preferably before they become too large.

DAUBENTON'S KALE
(AND OTHER PERENNIAL KALES)
(see page 57)

Brassica oleracea var. *ramosa*. Hardy biennial/perennial.

A delicious, perennial kale that was a Victorian favourite, growing into a plant that can easily make 1.5m high and wide and with all the classic green, bright flavour of a mid-green kale. Easy to grow, highly productive, and seems to be a little more robust in the face of the cabbage white butterflies than many.

VARIETIES: Other varieties to try include the very sweet 'Sutherland' kale, 'East Friesian Palm' kale and 'Walking Stick' kale, which can reach more than 3m tall.

STARTING OFF: Source plants from a good supplier. Daubenton's can be easily propagated from side shoots throughout the growing season.

POSITION: Perennial kales need a good fertile soil.

SPACING: This depends on variety but, as a general rule, space around 1m apart.

PRODUCTIVITY/EFFICIENCY: Once established, Daubenton's kale is both easily productive for years and requires little effort.

GROWING: Give an annual mulch of compost.

POTENTIAL PROBLEMS: Net against pigeons and butterflies if they are a problem in your area.

HARVEST: Pick leaves as required throughout the year, but they are particularly valuable through the winter and early spring months.

DAYLILIES

Hemerocallis species. Hardy perennial.

A glorious, early flowering plant, of which all parts are edible. We use the leaves and flowers most - shredded leaves add fresh punch to salads, and the flowers are superb raw, as tempura, in salads or in soups where they are traditionally used as a thickener. Their flavour is green, fresh and peppery - more intense in the reds than the yellows/oranges. As their name suggests, the trumpet blooms only last for a day, so pick them in the afternoon, safe in the knowledge that they are about to fade in any case. Although all parts can be eaten, a piece of advanced horticultural advice: leave the roots where they belong - under the soil - as lifting them kills the plant.

VARIETIES: There are a multitude of species and varieties to grow. You could try *H. lilioasphodelus* for an early yellow flower or 'Sammy Russell' for a red flower. *Hemerocallis fulva* enthusiastically colonises any ground given to it.

STARTING OFF: Source plants from a good supplier or lift and divide established plants in spring or autumn.

POSITION: Tolerant of most soils and prefer full sun.

SPACING: 30–45cm apart, depending on variety.

PRODUCTIVITY/EFFICIENCY: With careful choice of cultivars you can harvest shoots, buds and flowers from spring to early autumn.

GROWING: Clumps may need dividing every 3 years or so.

POTENTIAL PROBLEMS: Pick off and burn any unusually swollen buds that refuse to open to deter the Hemerocallis gall midge. Protect from slugs and snails early in the year.

HARVEST: Pick young leaves in spring, flower stems when no more than 12cm long, and the flowers that follow when they are fully open.

EARTH CHESTNUT

Bunium bulbocastanum. Also known as: great pignut and pignut, though not to be confused with the widely foraged *Conopodium majus*, which is also known as pignut. Hardy perennial.

A relatively small (60cm each way) perennial vegetable with feathered leaves and white summer flowers. Leaves, flowers and roots are all edible – the green parts carrying a lovely parsley flavour and are best eaten fresh, while the sweet chestnut-flavoured roots need roasting or boiling before eating. Allow some of the flowers to remain unpicked and collect the seed in autumn – it has a similar flavour to cumin and can be used in the same way.

VARIETIES: No named varieties available.

STARTING OFF: You can sow seed in modules under cover in spring, potting on once before planting out, or source plants from a specialist supplier.

POSITION: Moist, well-drained soil in full sun.

SPACING: 50cm apart.

PRODUCTIVITY/EFFICIENCY: A versatile plant, using leaves as a salad ingredient, seeds as a spice or the roots during winter.

GROWING: Little maintenance required, but plants tend to live for only around 5 years, so it can be an idea to save a little seed to sow the following year.

POTENTIAL PROBLEMS: Generally pest and disease free.

HARVEST: Pick leaves throughout the growing season, cut flower stalks in autumn for drying the seed, and dig the tubers during winter.

EGYPTIAN WALKING ONION

Allium proliferum. A type of tree onion. Hardy perennial.

If you've a little patience to allow them to establish, walking onions will give you plenty in return. Early in spring they throw up tubular leaves to pick as chives. Any you allow to grow on can be pulled off as spring onions. Allow some to develop and small bulbils (mini-onions) will form on the end of the leaves. Pick some as they grow if you like, allowing others to grow on - as they do, they'll weigh down the leaves, bending them until the bulbils touch the ground, where they will root and start the whole process off again - hence 'walking' around whatever space you allow them. Late in the season, the mother plant will have delicious shallot-like onions at its base - pick some, leaving the rest to provide the engine room for the following year. That's four delicious and different harvests from one perennial plant.

VARIETIES: No named varieties available.

STARTING OFF: Sow bulbils in small pots in spring or autumn.

POSITION: A reasonably drained soil in full sun, though they tolerate some shade.

SPACING: 30cm apart.

PRODUCTIVITY/EFFICIENCY: You can eat the onion bulbs that multiply at the base, leaves and bulbils. The onions will gently reproduce if given a weed-free bed.

GROWING: Needs very little maintenance and will travel around.

POTENTIAL PROBLEMS: Slugs – deal with them as you like.

HARVEST: Pick bulbils from the top in spring when young and tender or later in the year when big enough to bother with peeling. These late ones can be dried for storage. Leaves can be picked at any time of year but don't over-harvest. Dig up to harvest the bulbs but don't forget to replant one.

ENDIVE

Cichorium endivia. Hardy biennial.

I don't grow endive every year but look forward to them very much when I do. A few of their bitter leaves in a mixed leaf salad adds a little zippiness that sets off the plainer leaves beautifully. But I like them best cooked face down in a hot pan with a few spoonfuls of olive oil and too much salt and pepper, until they wilt into a blond sweet-bitter wig.

VARIETIES: There are escarole types that are broad-leaved and hardy, and frisée types with frizzy leaves, which are happier in summer and autumn. 'Cornet de Bordeaux' will happily stand the winter; 'Blonde Full Heart' is excellent for hearts and 'Fine de Louvier' for leaves. 'Cuor d'Oro' blanches itself.

STARTING OFF: Depending on variety sow in modules from April and plant out after first frosts, or sow direct from May to midsummer.

POSITION: Happy in most soils but escarole types, in particular, need reasonable drainage.

SPACING: 30cm apart.

PRODUCTIVITY/EFFICIENCY: Endive can be sown as a cut-and-come-again crop, ready in under 7 weeks; otherwise it takes 3 months for a harvest.

GROWING: Little maintenance needed other than watering in a dry patch.

POTENTIAL PROBLEMS: Very few but check for slugs on any that you are blanching.

HARVEST: Blanch endive to make them less bitter by covering with an upturned pot for 3 weeks, with stones covering the holes. Cut entire heads by slicing through the stalk at ground level.

FLORENCE FENNEL

Foeniculum vulgare var. *azoricum*. A hardy perennial usually grown as an annual.

The glassy, firm bulbs of Florence fennel develop best in sunny, airy spots in a sandy, fertile soil. Of those conditions, I can rely only on 'fertility' in Devon, but don't let similar limitations put you off - the bulbs you grow may look a little elongated compared with the ones in the shops but their flavour will be undiminished.

VARIETIES: 'Romanesco' and 'Finale' are reliable, delicious and bolt resistant.

STARTING OFF: Sow in modules under cover from April to July and plant outside from May. You can sow direct from May to July (or August for undercover crops). Sowing every 2–3 weeks will give you a good succession.

POSITION: Sunny and warm in a good and well-drained soil.

SPACING: 30cm apart.

PRODUCTIVITY/EFFICIENCY: Fennel will occupy space for 10–15 weeks and while not hugely productive, it is packed with flavour.

GROWING: Keep weed free and don't allow the soil around to dry out. A good mulch will help with this.

POTENTIAL PROBLEMS: Few problems but slugs may have a nibble.

HARVEST: Cut the stem when the bulbs have swelled to a good size any time from late July through to November. Cover the stem with soil for a secondary crop of small shoots and don't forget that any thinnings are delicious too.

FRENCH BEANS

Phaseolus vulgaris. Half-hardy annual.

French beans are ever-present in most kitchen gardens - steadily and unspectacularly, they fill baskets every day or two from midsummer into early autumn. I say unspectacularly, but look at them with fresh eyes: their easy climbing habit, beautiful flowers (they were once grown as ornamentals) with the dangling pods to follow - they are as extraordinary as they are productive.

VARIETIES: French beans come in any combination of dwarf or climbing, flat or round and coloured purple, yellow or green. Try 'Rocquencourt' and 'Purple Teepee' for round pods, or 'The Prince' or 'Nassau' for flat pod dwarf varieties. 'Eva' (yellow) and 'Blue Lake Climbing' (purple) are fabulous climbers. Good varieties for drying include 'Cannellino' or 'Lazy Housewife'.

STARTING OFF: Sow in small batches (they are heavy croppers) in 9cm pots in April (March if harvesting under cover) and plant out after the first frosts. Do 2 more sowings, 6 weeks apart, for a steady supply. You can use dwarf beans for earliest and latest sowings, as these mature quickly and can be easily protected with a cloche or fleece.

POSITION: Sunny, sheltered spot on a reasonable soil.

SPACING: 20–30cm apart, depending on variety.

PRODUCTIVITY/EFFICIENCY: Many beans are produced over a long period of time from June into October.

GROWING: Keep weed free, water while the pods develop and give climbers something to twine themselves up.

POTENTIAL PROBLEMS: Aphids can be an issue as can slug damage on young plants.

HARVEST: Pick when young and tender for the best flavour and texture – it will encourage the plant to produce more pods. For drying, leave beans on the plant until they rattle, then pick, shell and leave to dry on a flat surface indoors for another couple of days.

GARLIC

Allium sativum. Hardy perennial.

As much as I love regular bulbs of garlic, I grow more than half of my garlic to use early on in one form or another. Hardneck varieties produce stalks (scapes) that grow quickly in early summer – cut them while the flower is thin, closed and tear-shaped, for one of the harvests of the year. It is like garlic-flavoured asparagus. Hardneck varieties don't store well, so, as well as using the stalks, we tend to use the bulb as green garlic – picking them a few weeks before the individual cloves have formed. Roasted, they are mild, sweet and delicious. Softneck varieties tend to have a less complex, though stronger flavour and store well – we pick and dry these for using into winter.

VARIETIES: Before you choose a variety, consider how you want to eat it. Hardnecks should be used first – either for their leaves, as green garlic (see above) and as normal or dried bulbs. Softneck varieties store well and are best for using as you would shop-bought garlic.

'Picardy Wight' and 'Solent Wight' are two great-tasting softneck varieties that you can use well into winter, while 'Lautrec Wight' and 'Carcassonne Wight' are reliable and flavoursome hardnecks. Elephant garlic is more of a leek than a garlic, producing huge bulbs with a mild flavour – it is as tasty as it is impressive. Don't be tempted to grow from shop-bought garlic, as they are usually grown in warmer climates than Britain's and are more susceptible to viruses.

STARTING OFF: As garlic needs a certain amount of cold to induce it to bulb, plant by mid-February, ideally before Christmas. Separate the bulbs, discarding the tiny ones in the middle, and push individual cloves into the ground just below the surface with the pointy end up (10cm deep for Elephant garlic).

POSITION: Sun and free drainage.

SPACING: 20cm apart (25cm for Elephant garlic).

PRODUCTIVITY/EFFICIENCY: Garlic will be in the ground for 6–8 months but you have the possibility of scapes, green garlic and regular garlic bulbs. Many varieties store well for months, and it is one of the most transforming of flavours – just a little makes a great impact.

GROWING: Keep weed free. Tolerant of dry weather.

POTENTIAL PROBLEMS: Don't grow in the same place in successive years to reduce the risk of onion white rot and rust.

HARVEST: You can harvest garlic 'green' in May/early June for a mild flavour. The scapes can be harvested in early summer. Bulbs for drying will be ready in June or July once the leaves have turned yellow, with those planted before Christmas being a little larger and a little earlier than those planted later. Dry the bulbs in the sun for a few days and then store somewhere cool.

GARLIC CRESS

Peltaria alliacea. Hardy perennial.

One of the first and therefore most welcome leaves to emerge in spring, garlic cress grows reliably, with no attention, and adds punch and beauty to a spring salad when there's not much else to choose from. Pick the slim leaves early – as soon as the weather warms up they'll flower and bitterness follows. They make a fine pesto.

VARIETIES: No named varieties available.

STARTING OFF: Sow the seed in modules in spring or autumn and plant out in summer, or source as a young plant.

POSITION: Tolerant of most soils but likes some light shade. Plant in a permanent position.

SPACING: 20cm apart.

PRODUCTIVITY/EFFICIENCY: Can provide leaves most of the year.

GROWING: Will tolerate reasonable neglect.

POTENTIAL PROBLEMS: Generally untroubled.

HARVEST: Pick the leaves as desired. They are best between autumn and spring, becoming a little bitter over the summer when flowering. Happily, you can eat the flowers too.

GARLIC MUSTARD

Alliaria petiolata. Also known as: hedge garlic and Jack-by-the-hedge, due to its liking for growing exactly there. Hardy biennial.

A delicious, tall, nettle-like plant, with small white and yellow flowers, found in hedgerows, woodlands and riversides – anywhere where there's a good moist soil. Although it resembles a few wild plants, its bright green, heart-shaped leaves smell of garlic, distinguishing it from the others. A great leafy green for stir-fries and sides, and just the best in a cheese sandwich.

VARIETIES: No named varieties available.

STARTING OFF: Sow seed in modules from May to July and plant out when the roots are showing.

POSITION: Happy in most soils. Some shade preferred.

SPACING: 30cm apart.

PRODUCTIVITY/EFFICIENCY: This plant provides you with several crops over a reasonably long season. The young leaves are good raw. As they become older and hotter, they are better cooked. The seeds can be used as a peppery spice.

GROWING: Little maintenance needed.

POTENTIAL PROBLEMS: Generally pest and disease free.

HARVEST: You can start picking the young leaves in spring for salads and, later in the summer, use them in cooking. Harvest the seeds in summer.

GLOBE ARTICHOKES

Cynara scolymus. Hardy perennial.

It must have taken a hungry person to investigate the spiky armour of a globe artichoke in search of sustenance, yet somewhere underneath that threatening exterior lies culinary heaven. Harvested small, the immature flowers can be stripped of petals to reveal a pale, oval centre. Cut off the base to remove any petal remnants, then in half lengthways – remove any hint of fluffy choke from within. Immerse in acidulated water if not using immediately. Larger artichokes should be tackled in one of two ways. To demolish them in the classic 'French' style, boil them for 15–45 minutes (depending on size) and serve whole with a vinaigrette – peel off each of the petals, dip in the dressing and scrape the pad of succulent flesh from the petal with your teeth. To extract the heart for preserving or cooking, lay the artichoke on its side and use a bread knife to slice through the petals about 4cm from the base. Remove the petal stubs and any remnants. Ease out the fluffy immature flower (the choke) from the centre and discard. You are left with the heart. Either sauté or poach in a little wine and/or water until tender.

VARIETIES: 'Gros Vert de Laon', 'Violetta di Chioggia' and 'Violet de Provence' are classic and delicious varieties. 'Green Globe' is slightly hardier.

STARTING OFF: Growing from seed will give slightly variable results and takes time, so consider planting offsets/young plants. Sow seed in 9cm pots in spring and pot on once before planting out. Offsets can be taken from established plants in April by digging up and gently separating the newer groups of leaves that have developed at the base. Plant these straight away.

POSITION: Full sun and good drainage in a permanent position.

SPACING: Around 1.2m apart.

PRODUCTIVITY/EFFICIENCY: A relatively large space is taken up compared to the size of crop you get, but very low maintenance and any artichokes left to flower will be loved by the bees.

GROWING: Very little care needed. Replace plants every 3 or 4 years with some of the offsets they have produced.

POTENTIAL PROBLEMS: Slugs can bother small plants but otherwise trouble free.

HARVEST: Small side-heads on 'Violet de Provence' can be harvested as early as May before any choke has developed. Cut the plant to the base for another crop around 2 months later.

Otherwise, cut off the larger heads when plump and the scales tight between July and August.

GOOD KING HENRY

Chenopodium bonus-henricus. Hardy perennial.

Good King Henry has more noms-de-plume than Carlos the Jackal - poor man's asparagus and Lincolnshire spinach among them - which hints at its many uses. Its spears, leaves and flower buds are all equally, if differently, delicious. The spikes make for a wonderful pre-asparagus harvest in early spring - just cut them at 15-20cm and treat as you would asparagus. The leaves make a great spinach substitute, and the flower buds are amazing cooked in butter and garlic. A perennial that's as tough as old boots and with a long season of generosity.

VARIETIES: Generic.

STARTING OFF: Sow in modules under cover in March or sow direct.

POSITION: Prefers a reasonable amount of shade with only a couple of hours' full sun during the day. Avoid sandy or water-logged soils.

SPACING: 30cm for good ground cover, which will help to suppress weeds.

PRODUCTIVITY/EFFICIENCY: A delicious and productive perennial, and easy to grow.

GROWING: Allow plants to establish without harvesting any in their first year, building themselves up for years of delicious productivity.

POTENTIAL PROBLEMS: None.

HARVEST: Good King Henry will produce spikes early in the spring – cut them just below the soil level when young and tender – and leaves throughout the growing season, with the flower buds in summer.

GROUND NUT

Apios americana. Also known as: the potato bean. A tuberous, climbing hardy perennial.

A lively climber with beautiful, chocolate-coloured flowers and really tasty tubers - like nutty potatoes in flavour though more like yams in texture. I like them best roasted, though they can be fried or boiled, as you would potatoes. It can be slow to start growing in spring, but once underway there's no stopping it.

VARIETIES: Named varieties are increasingly available, all of which taste the same to my taste buds but they do yield a little more than the generic.

STARTING OFF: Source tubers from a specialist supplier or prop-agate by potting up or planting out tubers from established plants.

POSITION: Prefers moist but well-drained soil and is tolerant of reasonable amounts of shade.

SPACING: Around 30cm apart.

PRODUCTIVITY/EFFICIENCY: Takes up little space as it can be planted next to small trees or shrubs up which it likes to climb. As it is a nitrogen fixer, it improves the fertility of the soil as it grows.

GROWING: Give them a structure – even just a few canes – to climb up. Allow to establish for a few years after planting before harvesting some of the tubers.

POTENTIAL PROBLEMS: Generally disease free, but mice may go for the tubers if left over winter, so protect.

HARVEST: The tubers are around 5cm in diameter and can be harvested at any time of year, though you will upset the growing plant less if you pick them in autumn or winter. Remember to leave some tubers in place for the plant to regrow.

HOPS

Humulus lupulus. Deciduous perennial climber.

Apart from enriching some of my favourite ales, hops make a really good vegetable – with the young nutty shoots taking to a quick steaming very well. I tend to eat them as a simple side veg with olive oil, or as part of a stir-fry. They look beautiful too, scrambling over an arch or other structure, offering shade to plants beneath.

VARIETIES: You could try 'East Kent Golding', which climbs to around 6m. Or, for an easier-to-reach hop, try 'First Gold' that won't reach half that.

STARTING OFF: Source young plants from a good supplier, or take root cuttings or divide plants in spring for best results.

POSITION: Prefers any humus-rich soil and sun or semi-shade.

SPACING: Plants will reach around 1.5m in width.

PRODUCTIVITY/EFFICIENCY: Growing up through existing trees or trellises means hops take up little space, providing you with greens in the spring and cones for beer-making in the autumn.

GROWING: Either prune back to 50cm or so after harvesting or leave old stems for the new ones to climb up.

POTENTIAL PROBLEMS: Aphids can be a nuisance in summer, but generally pest and disease free.

HARVEST: Pick young shoots in spring for cooking, allowing some to grow on and survive. Cones (mature flowers) can be harvested for beer as they ripen in autumn. They are ripe when they have a strong 'hoppy' aroma and leave yellow lupulin powder on your fingers when you touch them.

HOSTA

Hosta species (see below). Hardy perennial.

A favourite not only of the slugs, but also much of Asia and increasingly inquisitive eaters in the UK. This succulent, usually grey-green plant is widely grown as an ornamental, with most unaware that many Hosta species are also edible. The emerging shoots are very good harvested in spring and steamed quickly, with butter and pepper.

VARIETIES: *H. sieboldiana* are large-leaved and you could try 'Big Daddy', 'Bressingham Blue' or 'Elegans'. The flowers and flower buds of *H. fortunei* are reputedly the most delicious.

STARTING OFF: Source plants from a good supplier or divide established plants in autumn or winter.

POSITION: A shady spot with moist soil.

SPACING: Depending on variety space 30–90cm apart. Err on the close side if you want good ground cover.

PRODUCTIVITY/EFFICIENCY: Hostas can take a few years to

establish but will be productive year after year. Little effort, other than encouraging a healthy population of frogs and other slug predators.

GROWING: Little maintenance needed.

POTENTIAL PROBLEMS: Protect from slugs when young in whatever way you see fit.

HARVEST: Harvest the hostons (rolled-up leaves) as they emerge in spring by snapping off at the base from the outside of the plant. Younger hostons need less cooking and can be lightly fried, whilst older, loosely furled hostons will need boiling briefly. The leaf-scales at the base of the hoston are slightly bitter and best removed. Allow the shoots that come up to replace those harvested to grow on and keep the plant alive.

JERUSALEM ARTICHOKE

Helianthus tuberosus. Hardy perennial.

Along with celeriac, these egg-sized tubers shout their subterranean origins in their hearty earthiness more than any other underground harvest. They are perhaps the easiest vegetable to grow: plant them once and any you leave unharvested will regrow the following year. They are one of the most generous plants too – cut its sunflowers for the house in summer, lift the tubers through winter and cut the tall stalks and leafy growth to compost as you harvest. And the flowers will attract plenty of beneficial insects to your garden. Jerusalem artichokes contain inulin, which isn't readily broken down by the body – this can cause 'interesting' results, but the body often quickly builds a tolerance and effects are diminished. Wonderful roasted, when they collapse a little and take on the flavours around them, or as the basis of a soup or risotto.

VARIETIES: 'Fuseau' is the least knobbly (hence easiest to peel) and highest yielding but 'Gerard' is said to have a smokier flavour if that appeals.

STARTING OFF: Jerusalem artichokes are perennial so find a permanent spot and plant tubers 15cm deep.

POSITION: Sunny with reasonable drainage.

SPACING: Around 60cm apart.

PRODUCTIVITY/EFFICIENCY: High-yielding crop requiring very little attention, though appreciative of the odd mulch with compost in spring.

GROWING: They make very tall plants producing beautiful yellow sunflower-like flowers in late summer. Their height and mass of growth make a good summer windbreak.

POTENTIAL PROBLEMS: None.

HARVEST: Jerusalem artichokes don't store well so dig as needed from October to February. Leave a few tubers in the ground for next year's supply.

KAI LAN

Brassica oleracea var. *alboglabra*. Also known as: Chinese broccoli, Chinese kale, gai-lan or kailaan. Hardy perennial.

In looks as well as flavour, kai lan looks very much like a cross between asparagus and sprouting broccoli and, depending on when you harvest and how you grow it, it is either one of the tastiest little-known harvests or a tough waste of time. The secret is to cut the growth while young and lush rather than let it become too leggy and woody. Get it right and you'll have succulent asparagus-crossed-with-sprouting-broccoli; leave it too long, and you'll have something with all the flavour and tenderness of a pencil. Unsurprisingly, eat it as you would asparagus or sprouting broccoli.

VARIETIES: No named varieties available.

STARTING OFF: Sow in modules under cover in February/March, for planting out as soon as the roots are showing. Sow again from July to September, direct if you prefer.

POSITION: Full sun in a composted and reasonably drained soil.

SPACING: 30–40cm apart.

PRODUCTIVITY/EFFICIENCY: Early sowings are ready to pull whole in 20 days or so. Later ones can be cut several times from around 2 months after sowing. Kai lan is a perennial and if you want to treat it as such, cut it back to 5cm in late autumn and allow to regrow in spring.

GROWING: Keep weed free and watered in dry weather.

POTENTIAL PROBLEMS: Fleece against flea beetle, butterflies and pigeons if they are a problem.

HARVEST: Leaves, stems and flowers are all edible. Pull up whole plants from early sowings and use all parts – these are likely to run to seed too quickly for you to use as cut-and-come-agains. For seed sown after midsummer cut the stems a few centimetres above the ground when 15–20cm tall and before they flower. You should be able to cut the stems twice more.

KALE

Brassica oleracea var. *acephala*. Hardy biennial, mostly grown as an annual.

Kale comes in as many distinctive and delicious varieties as tomatoes and chillies do, encouraging the gardener to try at least three or four. 'Red Russian' is my favourite, picked early, small and sweet for salads. This joins the dark, iron-y 'Cavolo Nero' for summer-into-autumn leaves with the substance to stand up to olive oil, chillies and garlic. 'Redbor' is a beautiful winter Leaf, adding colour and variety to the other two. There are many perennial kales to be found - 'Sutherland' is the sweetest of the ones I've tried.

VARIETIES: 'Red Russian', 'Redbor' and 'Cavolo Nero' are each delicious and distinct from each other. 'Sutherland' kale is very sweet. 'Daubenton's' kale (see page 37) is one of a number of fine perennial forms, as are 'East Friesian Palm' kale and 'Walking Stick' kale, both growing to an impressive height.

STARTING OFF: Sow seed in modules under cover from February to early August, depending on variety, potting on into 9cm pots. Plant out when 10–15cm tall. You can sow direct from April. Sowings made before May will give you a summer crop and those after, an autumn/winter one.

POSITION: Tolerant of some shade and an exposed site but soil should have reasonable drainage.

SPACING: 30–80cm apart, depending on variety and whether you plan to pick leaves when small.

PRODUCTIVITY/EFFICIENCY: Kales are productive over a long period of time and provide greens when little else is around. The immature flowers also make good eating.

GROWING: Keep weed free and don't allow to dry out.

POTENTIAL PROBLEMS: Fleece against flea beetle, butterflies and pigeons if they are a problem. Crop rotation will help deter clubroot.

HARVEST: Pick individual leaves of summer kale when small and sweet and as required from autumn/winter plants.

KOHLRABI

Brassica oleracea var. *gongylodes*. Hardy biennial, mostly grown as an annual.

Very possibly top of the 'What on earth do I do with that?' vegetable list. In the days before I found some excellent recipes for it, I remember using a few for a particularly close game of boules in the River Cottage kitchen garden. These days, while I'm still happy to tennis-racket any slug-ruined kohlrabi into the pig pen, the best of the harvest goes into remoulade and coleslaw, and also gratins with whichever of the green leaves are flourishing.

VARIETIES: 'Azur Star' is great for quick-growing roots, 'Gigant' for a large size and winter storage, and 'Luna' for sweet baby roots.

STARTING OFF: Sow in modules under cover from February to August, planting out as soon as its roots are showing.

POSITION: A sunny site with reasonable drainage.

SPACING: 25–30cm apart.

PRODUCTIVITY/EFFICIENCY: Crops can be ready in as little as 5 weeks.

GROWING: Keep weed free and watered in dry weather.

POTENTIAL PROBLEMS: Fleece against flea beetle, butterflies and pigeons if they are a problem for you. Crop rotation will help deter clubroot.

HARVEST: Pull kohlrabi as soon as it reaches the required size. Winter crops can withstand light frosts so dig up and store in paper sacks if you want to use over the winter. The leaves are also edible.

LEEKS

Allium ampeloprasum var. *porrum.* Hardy biennial, mostly grown as an annual.

With every year that passes, I grow more leeks. Their combination of fresh green flavour with sweet, mild onioniness wakes up everything from potatoes to red and white meat. They're relatively easy to grow well, and they add structure and height to the veg patch. Any left unharvested will sprout the most impressive flower heads late in the season – the mini-florets are very fine scattered through salads or in a mayonnaise.

VARIETIES: Early varieties include 'Hannibal' and 'Monstruoso de Carentan', with 'Saint Victor', 'Bleu de Solaise' and 'Musselburgh' good for later in the season. 'King Richard' is a good, very early variety that also makes for superb baby leeks.

STARTING OFF: Sow seed in modules under cover from February and plant out when 20cm tall using a dibber or narrow pen. Trim down the roots to a few centimetres before putting in the hole and water in but don't backfill the hole with soil – leave the leeks loose in the hole. Leeks can be sown outside from

March to early May. You could also try multi-sowing 4 seeds per module.

POSITION: Moisture-retentive soil in full sun.

SPACING: 15–25cm apart, depending on the size of leek required. For baby leeks, space at 1.5cm within the row and 15cm between rows. Space multi-sown leeks about 23cm apart.

PRODUCTIVITY/EFFICIENCY: Leeks take up little space and are very easy to grow, occupying the ground over autumn and winter.

GROWING: Keep weed free and watered in dry weather. Earth up for larger white parts.

POTENTIAL PROBLEMS: Use crop rotation to help prevent leek rust and fleece if leek moth is a problem in your area.

HARVEST: Dig as required, lifting baby leeks when around as thick as a pencil.

LETTUCE

Lactuca sativa. Hardy annual.

My teenage self probably ate less salad in a year than I do in most weeks now. While a lot of the reason for that must rest with me simply being a teenager, at least part is down to the terribly thin choice at the time. So many good lettuces are available in the shops these days, but the very best leaves are those that you grow yourself. I tend to grow half for cut-and-come-again leaves, growing the rest into hearting lettuces – many of them butterheads for summer salads. Do try some winter lettuces too – as well as salads, they make fine soups; try them with peas and a little lovage.

VARIETIES: Innumerable, with huge variety in looks, flavour and texture. Careful choice, some protection and different methods of harvesting can give you year-round lettuce. Try 'Buttercrunch' for a butterhead type that will withstand heat fairly well, 'Reine de Glace' or 'Pinokkio' for a bit of crunch, or 'Marvel of Four Seasons' and 'Winter Density' for lettuces to take you through the colder months. Most varieties can be planted for cut-and-come-again crops, but 'Red Oak Leaf' or 'Flashy Butter Oak' are particularly good.

STARTING OFF: Sow successively in modules under cover from January, and direct from March to September. Plant out as soon as the roots fill the modules (they may need some fleece or cloche protection). Sow seed in the evening during the warmer summer months, as seed needs cooler temperatures to germinate. Lettuce can bolt in hot weather so cut-and-come-again is a good option for this time of year.

POSITION: Ideally, a moisture-retentive but well-drained soil. Needs some shade in hotter months.

SPACING: 4–35cm apart, depending on harvesting method and variety.

PRODUCTIVITY/EFFICIENCY: Lettuces are quick from seed to harvest and a very efficient use of space, especially if grown as cut-and-come-again or harvested 'in the round'.

GROWING: Keep moist during dry weather and provide some shade in the hotter months, perhaps by growing on the north side of your bean poles.

POTENTIAL PROBLEMS: Your chosen slug and snail deterrents may be necessary.

HARVEST: For cut-and-come-again, harvest a couple of centimetres above the ground when a suitable size and leave to regrow, or pick individual leaves. By growing as a hearting lettuce but picking off individual leaves from the outside, you can harvest a single lettuce over a very long period.

MASHUA

Tropaeolum tuberosum. A herbaceous climber that is borderline hardy.

Like the potato, mashua originates from South America, and is similarly mighty fine to eat. Treat the tubers as you would most underground harvests - boil, roast or fry - to bring out their very gentle aniseed and pepperiness. Peel large tubers before cooking. The leaves are very similar in look and taste to nasturtiums, and the flowers are also edible: try both in salads. Above ground, it is a perennial climber that will scramble across the ground if given nothing to latch on to.

VARIETIES: Try *T. tuberosum pilifera* for white tubers and fiery orange flowers or *T. tuberosum* 'Ken Aslet' for early flowers and yellowy-red flowers.

STARTING OFF: Source tubers from a good supplier or pot up tubers from an existing plant.

POSITION: Full sun in a moist but well-drained soil.

SPACING: 40cm apart.

PRODUCTIVITY/EFFICIENCY: Leaves, flowers and tubers of this beautiful climber are edible. Very productive over a long period.

GROWING: Lift tubers before the cold weather and store in moist sand or sawdust over winter.

POTENTIAL PROBLEMS: Generally pest and disease free. Late frosts can knock back new growth, but they will usually recover. A long summer is needed for good-sized tubers.

HARVEST: Leave tubers in the ground for as long as possible to allow them to swell, but dig up before the ground freezes. Leaves and flowers can be harvested throughout the growing season and the seeds (like nasturtiums) can be picked in autumn and used like capers.

MEXICAN TREE SPINACH

Chenopodium giganteum. Hardy annual.

One of the prettiest leafy plants in the garden, Mexican tree spinach is one of those plants you need only grow once to have a friend for life. A close relative of fat hen (commonly thought of as a weed), it is one of the earliest leaves to emerge in spring - and is likely to do so randomly, within wind-blowing distance of its parent, if you let it go to seed. Growing to more than 2m, and with leaves that carry splashes of vivid pink that intensify the hotter the sun, Mexican tree spinach can be used as you would spinach - in salads or wilted in any number of main courses.

VARIETIES: No named varieties.

STARTING OFF: Sow in modules in March under cover and plant out as soon as the roots have filled them. Sow direct outside when the soil is warming up.

POSITION: Full sun and tolerant of most soils.

SPACING: Plants will grow to around 1.5m if given enough space, but grow 5–10cm apart for a cut-and-come-again crop.

PRODUCTIVITY/EFFICIENCY: A small patch of cut-and-come-again will give you several harvests.

GROWING: Little maintenance required.

POTENTIAL PROBLEMS: Very trouble free.

HARVEST: Pick individual leaves from large plants or cut whole shoots when around 20cm tall if grown closely together, allowing them to regrow for a second or third harvest.

MIBUNA

Brassica rapa Japonica Group. Hardy annual.

Greener in colour and flavour than mizuna, mibuna sits ever so slightly more on the brassica side of things too. I was never that taken with it until I tried 'Green Spray' – an altogether fresher variety, that's pretty hardy and reliable. I prefer its more balanced flavour and that, for some reason, its leaves seem to avoid the flea beetle a little better than regular mibuna. A great salad leaf when small; when larger, use wilted in place of spinach.

VARIETIES: Few named varieties but try 'Green Spray'.

STARTING OFF: For an under-cover crop, sow from mid-February to mid-April in modules, planting as soon as the roots are showing. Sow outside after mid-June, as it will bolt if sown in the approach to midsummer.

POSITION: Moisture-retentive and well-drained soil. It will tolerate some shade.

SPACING: 25cm apart.

PRODUCTIVITY/EFFICIENCY: Each plant produces masses of long, narrow leaves, which you can cut 3 or 4 times.

GROWING: Little maintenance required.

POTENTIAL PROBLEMS: Flea beetle shouldn't be a problem for sowings made after midsummer.

HARVEST: Cut leaves about 3cm above the ground as required. They will re-sprout and can be cut and harvested 3 or 4 more times in this way.

MICROLEAVES

Any midsummer birthday cards I get usually end up cluttering the dining table because the window sills (where my daughter likes to put cards) are taken up with lengths of guttering. A few inches of compost in each is all that's needed to nurse any of these punchy vegetables and herbs, which can be picked at just 5-6cm tall. Snipped just above the surface or pulled free and brushed clean of compost, many of the best have an intensity and cleanliness of flavour far superior to their full-grown version. And they're ready as quickly as a week after sowing in summer. Wonderful strewn in leafy salads, as a small salad of their own, or to add zip to all kinds of recipes, especially baked fish.

VARIETIES: Try fennel, rocket, radish, chervil, sorrel, coriander, nasturtium and any of the oriental leaves such as 'Red Giant' mustard or mizuna.

STARTING OFF: Sow in a seed tray or guttering throughout the year.

POSITION: Somewhere warm and light like a window sill or polytunnel.

SPACING: Sow thickly.

PRODUCTIVITY/EFFICIENCY: A very quick harvest from a small space, and (with the right choice of micros) offering huge flavour from a small harvest.

GROWING: Keep the compost lightly moist.

POTENTIAL PROBLEMS: None.

HARVEST: Microleaves will be ready from 7–20 days, depending on what you are growing and the time of year. Harvest by lifting and brushing free of compost, or cutting, when no taller than 7cm.

MIZUNA

Brassica rapa var. *Japonica.* Hardy annual.

One of the easiest oriental leaves to love, mizuna looks like a more deeply incised version of rocket, marrying a gentle pepperiness with fresh green flavour. You'll probably have eaten plenty of it, as it makes up one of the key components of many salad bags because it takes very well to cut-and-come-again harvesting and grows reliably for much of the year. As with most oriental leaves, pick them small for salads and use the larger, more peppery leaves in place of spinach.

VARIETIES: Few named varieties but try 'Mizuna Purple' for purple-tinged leaves or 'Broad Leaf, for a bolt-resistant mizuna.

STARTING OFF: Sow in modules under cover from mid-February to mid-April, planting out as soon as the roots are showing.

Direct sow from mid-June to September. If sown from May to early June, plants will bolt.

POSITION: Full sun or light shade in a moisture-retentive but well-drained soil.

SPACING: 15cm apart for cut-and-come-again leaves and around 25cm for larger leaves for stir-frying.

PRODUCTIVITY/EFFICIENCY: Ready to harvest in 4–6 weeks with 3–4 harvests possible from one plant if growing as cut-and-come-again.

GROWING: Ensure soil around plants is kept moist.

POTENTIAL PROBLEMS: If growing after midsummer flea beetle shouldn't be a bother, otherwise fleece against them.

HARVEST: Cut entire plant at the base if harvesting large leaves for stir-frying. For cut-and-come-again leaves, cut 3cm above the ground when around 10cm tall.

MOOLI

Raphanus sativus var. *longipinnatus*. Also known as: daikon or Chinese white radish. Hardy biennial.

A few years ago, I met Japanese grower Shige Takezoe who had dedicated a fair stretch of his polytunnel to his beloved mooli. He convinced me to try growing these long, pale radish again – I hadn't grown them well in the few years I'd tried – giving them the sunniest spot I could find and plenty of water. I owe him. Their crisp, fresh texture is really special and their radish brightness is altogether more pure and satisfying than many of the regular radishes you can grow. They're very fine used as you would regular radishes, but I especially like them lightly, briefly pickled.

VARIETIES: No named varieties.

STARTING OFF: Sow seed direct from late June to early September into well-prepared soil. Seed can be sown successionally for a continual supply of young roots.

POSITION: Likes a deep soil – moist but well-drained – and in full sun.

SPACING: Thin to 10cm apart within rows with 25cm between rows.

PRODUCTIVITY/EFFICIENCY: Great for a quick crop where summer veg have been lifted.

GROWING: Water during dry spells.

POTENTIAL PROBLEMS: Generally pest and disease free. Early sowings have greater risk of bolting.

HARVEST: Harvest baby mooli 7–8 weeks after sowing. Later sowings of mooli are harvested in November before the frosts and will keep for a week or so in the fridge.

MUSHROOMS

Many edible species. Perennial.

As summer slips into autumn and the weather gets wetter, you'll find (largely) bearded or be-hatted men sneaking off to closely guarded secret sites in the hope of finding delicious (as opposed to poisonous) fungi. Much fun it is too, but it is perfectly possible to grow mushrooms in the comfort of your own garden or even your home. More than that, you can tweak the conditions to make them just right for mushroom production for much more of the year than the wild harvest. Oyster mushrooms are a good first stop - an old book indoors or a bin bag of straw are all it takes for your first home-grown fungi.

VARIETIES: Shiitake, oyster, lion's mane, shaggy inkcap and Stropharia to name but a few.

STARTING OFF: Spawn usually comes in the form of grain or pegs. Refer to suppliers' instructions on how to start your chosen variety.

POSITION: Often on straw, bark chippings or hard or softwood logs. Refer to suppliers' instructions for your particular mushroom.

SPACING: Dependent on type of mushroom. Refer to suppliers' instructions.

PRODUCTIVITY/EFFICIENCY: Once started off, mushrooms can largely be left to their own devices. Depending on mushroom type they may crop over many months – or even years – if their food source is replenished.

GROWING: Refer to supplier for specifics of each variety.

POTENTIAL PROBLEMS: Employ your chosen slug deterrent.

HARVEST: This is often in autumn after a cool rain following a warm spell. Refer to information from your supplier for specifics.

NEW ZEALAND SPINACH

Tetragonia tetragonoides. Hardy evergreen perennial.

For some reason, perhaps best known to botanists, New Zealand spinach seems to dodge every ailment that besets regular spinach and other similar leafy greens. So its lightly glossy, gorgeous triangular leaves not only taste fabulous, they make you look like a champion gardener. It's a perennial that covers the ground quickly, retaining moisture and swamping out weeds but, alas, hard frosts see it off, so it'll only flourish all year round under cover in the warm.

VARIETIES: No named varieties.

STARTING OFF: Soak seed overnight to speed up germination. Sow in 9cm pots under cover around 3 weeks before the last frosts (6 weeks earlier if you are growing it under cover) and plant out after the last one.

POSITION: Full sun in moisture-retentive and well-drained soil.

SPACING: 30–45cm apart.

PRODUCTIVITY/EFFICIENCY: New Zealand spinach will be ready for harvesting around 2 months after sowing, forming a fairly spreading plant. From a single sowing you can harvest until the first frosts. A spinach that won't bolt.

GROWING: Water only in the driest weather.

POTENTIAL PROBLEMS: Generally pest and disease free.

HARVEST: Pick individual leaves and leaf tips throughout the growing season.

OCA

Oxalis tuberosa. Borderline hardy perennial.

Oca looks like a knobbly new potato and shares many of the qualities of an early potato - a lovely nuttiness and a firm texture, especially. But they differ in a number of crucial ways. Oca isn't susceptible to blight and neither does it turn green when exposed to the light – instead, its gentle just-harvested, lemony edge sweetens in the sun, giving you a range of flavours at the end of the season when they're ready to lift. Keep a few back to sow next year and you have an unbuyable harvest year after year for only the expense of starting in year one. I use them grated raw in salads as well as in most of the ways I do new potatoes.

VARIETIES: Usually sold as generic rather than named varieties, though tubers can be pink, yellow or white.

STARTING OFF: Start oca under cover in April by sowing one tuber per 9cm pot and plant them outside in May once the last frosts are over.

POSITION: Full sun in moisture-retentive and well-drained soil.

SPACING: 30–40cm apart.

PRODUCTIVITY/EFFICIENCY: Oca will occupy the ground for 6 months and can produce around half a kilo of tubers per plant. Needs little attention.

GROWING: Mulch to retain moisture around plants.

POTENTIAL PROBLEMS: Generally untroubled by pests and diseases.

HARVEST: Tubers form very late, so don't dig until a couple of weeks after the leaves have been killed off by frosts. If a hard frost is forecast, it will be worth protecting the soil to prevent the tubers from freezing.

ONIONS

Allium cepa. Hardy bulb.

Every year I grow fewer traditional onions – something has to give when you've only so much space and time, so it's the harvests that are relatively inexpensive and taste reasonably similar whether bought or grown that tend to get left off the list. The exceptions are red onions, which are often inexplicably pricey, and a short row of one or two white varieties that I change every year. The saved space is dedicated to shallots and a few trials of new flavours I've not grown before.

VARIETIES: 'Centurion' and 'White Ebenezer' are reliable and tasty white varieties; and 'Red Baron' and 'Red Electric' are fine red ones. Choose varieties well for flavour that's superior to most shop-bought onions.

STARTING OFF: Sow several seeds per module under cover in February/March and plant out when around 10cm tall, or sow direct in April. Plant sets from September to November or in March, pushing the set into the ground so that only the very tip is showing.

POSITION: Full sun in a well-drained, moisture-retentive soil.

SPACING: Spacing will determine onion size. 25cm apart for multi-sown modules. If sowing in rows, space 4–10cm apart within rows and 30cm between rows.

PRODUCTIVITY/EFFICIENCY: Onions can be occupying the ground from between 20 weeks for a spring set planting, and 40 weeks for autumn-sown seed.

GROWING: Onions dislike competition so keep weed free.

POTENTIAL PROBLEMS: Rotate to avoid onion downy mildew and white rot. Don't store any soft onions, as they may rot.

HARVEST: In dry weather pull up onions once their foliage has died down and lay out to dry for a couple of days, turning occasionally. Onions grown from seed in autumn don't store well.

OSTRICH FERN

Matteuccia struthiopteris. Also known as: shuttlecock fern and fiddlehead fern. Hardy perennial.

A delicious treat that's happiest growing in damp shade, where there is little else screaming for the space. Eat only the young emerging shoots – known as fiddleheads – which are crisp, with a fine flavour somewhere between asparagus and calabrese, but they must be cooked for at least 15 minutes or they can cause stomach upsets.

VARIETIES: The hard-to-source 'Jumbo' lives up to its name – growing to 2m.

STARTING OFF: Source plants from a good supplier or propagate by division in spring.

POSITION: Moist but well-drained neutral to acid soils. Prefers light shade.

SPACING: 60cm apart for good ground cover. Plants can reach 1.5m in height.

PRODUCTIVITY/EFFICIENCY: Plants will easily colonise the area they are given by spreading via rhizomes. They give an asparagus-flavoured treat when other greens are scarce.

GROWING: Little maintenance needed.

POTENTIAL PROBLEMS: Generally untroubled by pests and diseases.

HARVEST: Harvest the young shoots or 'fiddleheads' in spring when the leafy section is still tightly furled – they can be 20–50cm tall at this stage, although the lower part of the stem is likely to be tough and will need removing. Plants can be forced in the winter for an earlier crop. Wash and remove the hairs before cooking.

PARSNIP

Pastinaca sativa. Hardy biennial, mostly grown as an annual.

I eat a fair amount of parsnips through the winter, and while I can't hope to grow all of the pale tapering roots that I use, I usually sow a row or two because they seem to thrive so happily here. I'm easily flattered. Occasionally, I let some grow on for a second year, when they'll flower tall and beautiful - their umbel-liferous heads catching the eye and drawing in all manner of beneficial insects.

VARIETIES: 'Tender and True' and 'Gladiator' are delicious. 'Half Long Guernsey' is tasty, with good disease resistance.

STARTING OFF: Sow direct in March/April as the soil is warming up.

POSITION: Full sun on a sandy, well-worked soil.

SPACING: Sow in rows 30cm apart and thin to 15cm between plants. You can also grow parsnips closer together for smaller roots, which are good for summer harvesting.

PRODUCTIVITY/EFFICIENCY: Parsnips are in the ground for around 10 months of the year.

GROWING: Germination is erratic and slow. It's a good idea to sow with radish at the same time – by the time you harvest the radish, your parsnips should be showing.

POTENTIAL PROBLEMS: Root rot and canker can be a problem on heavier soils, so grow a resistant variety and avoid very early sowings.

HARVEST: Lift as desired after the first frosts.

PEAS

Pisum sativum. Hardy annual.

It's very hard to grow anywhere near all the peas you'll want to eat, but don't let that stop you from growing them – picked fresh from the plant and eaten before you've had chance to walk more than a few feet from it, they are the ultimate garden treat. I rarely cook those that I've grown – they're too good straight from the plant – and frozen peas are perfectly similar to home-grown peas when cooked. Growing your own also opens the door to pea shoots, and the finest sugar snap and mangetout varieties.

VARIETIES: Try 'Douce Provence' for a dwarf, hardy and productive pea for sowing year round or 'Alderman', 'Hurst Green Shaft' or 'Ne Plus Ultra' for a sweet, productive climbing pea. 'Markana' is good for an exposed site, or you could try 'Purple Podded Pea' for some colour. Sugar snap peas such as 'Sugar Ann' will give you some sweet crunch or try a mangetout variety such as 'Norli' or 'Weggisser'.

STARTING OFF: Timing depends on variety, so check the packet. Start under cover in root trainers or guttering for early crops, planting out when the plants are 10–15cm tall. Sow outside once the soil is warming up. Either sow little and often (every 2–3 weeks) or in larger quantities in spring, summer and autumn.

POSITION: A sunny spot with a moisture-retentive, free-draining soil.

SPACING: Direct sow peas 5cm deep, in trenches 20cm wide. Space peas at around 7cm apart, with 60–90cm between trenches. Plant out seedlings at similar spacing.

PRODUCTIVITY/EFFICIENCY: Peas produce over a long period of time if you keep picking. Climbing varieties will make more efficient use of space, particularly important if you're short of ground space. You can have crops from May to September.

GROWING: Little needed other than support. Twiggy hazel branches are best if you can get them. Leave roots in the ground when plants have gone over, as they are nitrogen rich and will break down to feed the soil.

POTENTIAL PROBLEMS: Mice like the seed and slugs the young plants. Start in root trainers to avoid the worst of this. Fleece against pigeons if they are a problem. Plants should outgrow pea and bean weevil attacks. Sow quick-growing peas early and late to avoid pea moth or grow mangetout varieties.

HARVEST: Pick pods whilst the peas inside are a good size but still young and succulent. Don't allow any pods to completely mature, as this will stop the plant from producing any more flowers/peas.

POTATOES

FIRST AND SECOND EARLIES

Solanum tuberosum. Half-hardy perennial, mostly grown as an annual.

The first handfuls of 'International Kidney', 'Belle de Fontenay' and the unromantically named 'BF15' make me ridiculously happy. Sweet, firm and cooked in just a few minutes, they are a spring-into-summer treat of which I never tire. They are rightly expensive in the shops too, so growing them saves a hatful of money.

VARIETIES: There is a huge variety of flavour, shape and colour available. Try first earlies 'Foremost', 'Epicure' and 'Lady Christl'. For second earlies (more productive and taking slightly longer to mature), try 'British Queen' or 'Yukon Gold' for an excellent chipper and roaster.

STARTING OFF: Chit potatoes for a few weeks to induce sturdy young shoots, by placing your seed potatoes on a tray, eye-side up, in a light place. Plant out in trenches or holes from mid-March, covered by around 10cm of soil. Alternatively, cover your potato bed with 8–10cm compost and top with mulch matting, cutting holes to plant through (big enough for leaves to emerge from) – this removes the need to dig trenches/holes or earth up (see 'spacing').

POSITION: A sunny site with well-drained soil.

SPACING: Variable, depending on the size of your chosen cultivars and how large you want your potatoes to grow. Plant 35cm apart along rows with 50cm between rows. You could also try a closer spacing if using the mulching method (see 'starting off').

I've tried planting at 30cm between tubers, neither mulching nor earthing up – just allowing the foliage to shade the tubers, and although smaller tubers result, the hassle of earthing up is avoided.

PRODUCTIVITY/EFFICIENCY: Earlies will be in the ground for around 4 months. The yields will not be as large as for maincrops and are best eaten soon after they have been dug.

GROWING: To prevent your tubers turning green, earth up or mulch with compost, leaf mould or similar when shoots are around 15cm tall and again before the leaves touch.

POTENTIAL PROBLEMS: Much fewer than maincrop potatoes – they are usually dug up before blight and slugs become a serious problem.

HARVEST: Most varieties of early potatoes are ready to harvest when they flower. Dig up as you want to eat them. Some varieties are suitable for baking and roasting if left in the ground and grown on.

POTATOES

MAINCROP

Solanum tuberosum. Half-hardy perennial, mostly grown as an annual.

For years, I grew pretty much only early varieties of potato, but recently I've been risking a row or two of maincrops to the scourge of blight. 'Mayan Gold' makes incredibles crisps and roast potatoes with the perfect blend of crisp shell and buttery centre, which is a huge incentive. But I've always loved 'Pink Fir

Apple' – perhaps too much, as I can't bear losing them to blight. On my head be it.

VARIETIES: Maincrop potatoes are the highest yielding and a huge choice is available to you. 'Cara' or purple-skinned 'Arran Victory' have creamy flesh for roasting and baking, or try 'Pink Fir Apple' for a maincrop waxy salad potato. 'Sarpo Mira' is the one for blight resistance – and growing it helps boost the commercial market for it, which means more potatoes grown without the huge chemical additives most come with.

STARTING OFF: Chit potatoes for a few weeks to induce sturdy young shoots, by placing your seed potatoes on a tray, eye-side up, in a light place. Plant out in trenches or holes from mid-March covered by around 10cm of soil. Alternatively, cover your potato bed with 8–10cm compost and top with mulch matting, cutting holes to plant through (big enough for leaves to emerge from) – this removes the need to dig trenches/holes or earth up (see below, 'spacing').

POSITION: A sunny site with well-drained soil.

SPACING: Variable, depending on the size of your chosen cultivars and how large you want your tubers to grow. Plant about 40cm apart if you are using a mulching method (see above, 'starting off'), or 35–45cm apart along rows and 65–75cm between rows if earthing up.

PRODUCTIVITY/EFFICIENCY: Maincrop potatoes will occupy the ground for around 5 months and will risk blight, but many varieties store over winter.

GROWING: To prevent your tubers turning green, earth up or mulch with compost, leaf mould or similar when shoots are around 15cm tall and again before the leaves touch.

POTENTIAL PROBLEMS: Maincrops are more susceptible to blight than early potatoes so grow a more resistant variety and cut leaves to the ground if blight hits, lifting them as soon as you can. Slugs living in the soil like tubers – a no-dig system can help here.

HARVEST: Dig up your potatoes when the foliage dies down, usually in August. If storing, keep only the perfect ones.

PURSLANE

WINTER AND SUMMER

Portulaca oleracea. Half-hardy annual. Also *Claytonia perfoliata*. Hardy annual.

Winter purslane is as tough as it appears delicate, being not only frost resistant but tolerating poor soils and shade. Leaves may be small but they are abundant and easily harvested – and they make especially welcome crop through winter. Delicious, crisp of texture and high in omega-3.

Summer purslane has a peppery edge to its flavour, and it is best used raw in salads, or steamed and very high in omega-3. Much less resilient than winter purslane, summer purslane is nevertheless perfectly productive in the heat of summer.

VARIETIES: No named varieties of either but there are golden and green forms of summer purslane, with golden purslane tasting a little more of lemon. Winter purslane is also known as claytonia and miner's lettuce.

STARTING OFF: Sow summer purslane successively from April to August (earlier and later if cropping in a tunnel). Sow winter purslane successively from June to September. The seed is very small so it is easiest sown direct very sparingly.

POSITION: Tolerant of most soils.

SPACING: Thin to 15cm apart.

PRODUCTIVITY/EFFICIENCY: A small patch will keep you in leaves for a considerable period.

GROWING: Little needed.

POTENTIAL PROBLEMS: Generally problem free but summer purslane is a half-hardy annual and won't tolerate frosts.

HARVEST: Pick shoot tips and individual leaves as required. The plant will send out side shoots for harvesting at a later date.

QUINOA

Chenopodium quinoa. Half-hardy annual.

Quinoa is a high-protein seed (although commonly thought of as a grain), cooked just like rice, with a couscous-like nutty flavour. It grows as a tall plant, like a spinach crossed with sweetcorn, its big flowers developing into seed-rich heads in the run up to harvesting. The seeds can be a number of colours – most commonly, yellow and red – and this bitter-coloured coating of saponins helps protect them from the birds' attentions. Soak them in water to remove the coating before cooking to avoid any soapiness.

VARIETIES: 'Temuco' and 'Rainbow' crop well in a damp climate due to their open seed heads.

STARTING OFF: Sow seed in modules under cover in early April, potting on once before planting out after the last frosts.

POSITION: Full sun in a moist but well-drained soil.

SPACING: 50cm apart. Plants can reach 2m tall in a good year.

PRODUCTIVITY/EFFICIENCY: Quinoa gives very high yields in relation to the space it takes up, occupying the ground from late May to late September.

GROWING: Provide support, as these are tall, shallow-rooted plants.

POTENTIAL PROBLEMS: Generally pest and disease free.

HARVEST: Quinoa is ready in September when the seeds are changing colour and come away easily from the plant when rubbed between your fingers. Cut the stems and hang up to dry out for a few days, then rub the seed heads between your hands whilst holding over a bowl or sheet. You will be left with a pile of quinoa and chaff, which needs spreading out to dry for a few more days. When dry, pour the seeds from one bowl to another outside when there is a light breeze. This blows away the chaff, leaving you with just the seed.

RADISH

Raphanus sativus. Hardy annual.

If you're starting off or in need of a quick return, sow radishes. They'll be ready in no time and reassure you that this growing lark really isn't so tricky. Home-grown radishes really are a very different prospect from those in the shops – pick them early, before any woodiness or all-out heat takes them over. They can be anywhere from cool to hot, crisp to sweet, depending on variety. They're also good sown in short-lived gaps between crops, being quick to harvest. Don't be too hasty to pull up any plants that go to seed – the seed pods are full of flavour.

VARIETIES: Try the classic white-tipped 'French Breakfast' or 'Scarlet Globe'. 'Icicle' is a long white radish, or try the yellow 'Szlata'. Mooli (see page 67) can be sown in late summer for a larger autumn/winter radish. 'Rat's Tail' has been specifically bred for its tasty pods.

STARTING OFF: Sow summer radish little and often outside from March to September. Sow thinly in rows that are 15cm apart or broadcast. Autumn mooli varieties should be sown in July or August.

POSITION: Full sun or partial shade on a moisture-retentive soil. Don't over-manure before sowing.

SPACING: Thin to around 2–3cm apart.

PRODUCTIVITY/EFFICIENCY: Radishes are ready to crop in about 4 weeks and can be sown around crops that take longer to reach maturity.

GROWING: Keep soil around radish moist to keep a nice steady growth and prevent them splitting.

POTENTIAL PROBLEMS: Very few.

HARVEST: Pull when roots are young and tender. Mooli can be dug as required through late summer, autumn and into winter. Pull the seed pods whenever they reach a size, flavour and texture you like.

RED VALERIAN

Centranthus ruber. Not to be confused with *Valeriana officinalis*, which is used medicinally. Hardy perennial.

I've only just started growing this gorgeous pink/red-flowered plant in the last couple of years, but I'm already hooked. The young leaves and shoots have a similar flavour to broad beans and are really good either in salads or as a side dish of their own. Easy to grow in well-drained conditions, it can even self-seed and remain evergreen in sheltered, sunny spots.

VARIETIES: Available only in its generic form although there is also white-flowered generic form.

STARTING OFF: Source plants from a good supplier or start from seed. Sow in spring in modules under cover, potting on once before planting out.

POSITION: Full sun in well-drained soil. Poor soils are tolerated. Valerian also grows well in walls and will do well in a container.

SPACING: 40cm apart.

PRODUCTIVITY/EFFICIENCY: Centranthus can provide leaves year-round in some milder areas where it is evergreen.

GROWING: Cut back flower heads if you prefer fresh new greens over attracting butterflies.

POTENTIAL PROBLEMS: Keep watered during dry weather to avoid the leaves becoming bitter whilst the plant is flowering.

HARVEST: Pick shoots in spring, and young leaves as desired throughout the year – though avoid any during extended dry spells as they can become bitter.

ROCKET

Rucola coltivata. Hardy annual.

Like pasta and duvets before it, rocket invaded our country at some point during the last series of Starsky & Hutch and now we can't imagine life without it. Fair enough: it is one of the most delicious and reliable salad leaves, it's easy to grow, and it's productive too - taking well to cut-and-come-again harvesting. It also makes a fine, punchy pesto.

VARIETIES: Wild rocket is very productive – growing steadily for months of repeat harvesting, and is the one to grow through the summer. Rucola runs to seed more quickly than wild rocket, so I tend to grow it for all but the hottest months.

STARTING OFF: Sow from February to October directly, avoiding May and June if you want to avoid any risk of bolting.

POSITION: Sun or partial shade in a moisture-retentive, well-drained soil.

SPACING: 5–15cm apart, depending on how large you want the leaves.

PRODUCTIVITY/EFFICIENCY: Rocket can be ready to eat in as little as 3 weeks and so can be sown at the base of other crops.

GROWING: Keep moist in dry weather. Grow in partial shade during hotter months.

POTENTIAL PROBLEMS: Fleece if flea beetle is a problem.

HARVEST: Cut leaves when young and tender at around 2cm above ground level, leaving them to regrow. Leave some to run to seed, as the flowers are edible too.

ROMANESCO

Brassica oleracea var. *Botrytis* 'Romanesco'. Hardy biennial, mostly grown as an annual.

Thought by some to be a kind of cauliflower, sometimes known as Italian broccoli, and many consider it a vegetable all of its own. I'm in the latter camp: its logarithmic pattern of self-replicating spirals is as uniquely beautiful as it is delicious. It's a reliable grower too - none of that 'pick it today or it's blown' nonsense you get with a cauliflower. Roast it with oil and garlic and/or shred finely and stir-fry with garlic, anchovy, chilli and olive oil for a fine pasta sauce.

VARIETIES: Usually sold as generic, but you may find 'Veronica' available.

STARTING OFF: Sow seed in modules under cover from February to May, potting on into 9cm pots and planting out when the roots are showing.

POSITION: Full sun in a well-drained, moisture-retentive soil that has been mulched with compost.

SPACING: Between 25–60cm apart, depending on the sized head you want.

PRODUCTIVITY/EFFICIENCY: Romanesco takes up a considerable space for around 4–5 months of the year, but they are reliable to grow and expensive to buy.

GROWING: Keep soil moist to avoid checking growth.

POTENTIAL PROBLEMS: Fleece against flea beetle, butterflies and pigeons if they are a problem for you. Use crop rotation and lime the soil if your brassicas have clubroot.

HARVEST: Harvest between August and January, cutting when the required size.

RUNNER BEANS

Phaseolus coccineus. Half-hardy perennial, mostly grown as an annual.

The mistake many make with runner beans is to cook them. If you're in any doubt about their marvellousness, take one of these long, flat, slender pods from the plant when it's no wider than your third finger and you'll find them sweet, crisp and full of life. I've genuinely never known anyone not be converted by their flavour and texture. Otherwise, pick them small, steam them briefly and be generous with the olive oil and garlic.

VARIETIES: 'Polestar', 'Kelvedon Marvel' and 'Scarlet Emperor' are delicious red-flowered varieties. 'Polestar' is one I've never known to go stringy. 'White Lady' has white flowers and 'Pickwick' is a short variety needing very little support, so it's good for an exposed site or container.

STARTING OFF: Sow under cover in April in root trainers, planting out after the last frosts. Sow direct from May to July.

POSITION: Sunny spot with well-composted, moisture-retentive soil.

SPACING: 15cm apart within the row and 60cm between rows for tall varieties. For block planting dwarf varieties allow 25–30cm apart in all directions.

PRODUCTIVITY/EFFICIENCY: Plants are very productive over a 3 month period. You can make a second sowing in early July for runners into autumn.

GROWING: Provide support for tall varieties and water well in dry weather to encourage more flowers and good fruit set.

POTENTIAL PROBLEMS: Plant marigolds and other insect-attracting flowers to draw in aphid predators. Buy seed from a good supplier to avoid halo blight. Birds can peck flowers off, but in my experience they rarely do.

HARVEST: Pick from 10–17cm, eating the smallest ones whole. By picking often you will keep the plant producing. Flowers are edible too, but you will not have so many beans. At the end of the season try letting the bean mature inside the pod for using like butter beans.

SALSIFY AND SCORZONERA

Tragopogon porrifolius. Hardy biennial, mostly grown as an annual.

If you grow carrots or parsnips (or are considering either), you also have to grow one of these two. As easy to grow as any other long root vegetable, salsify and scorzonera both taste of globe artichokes, a little of asparagus and have something of the sea about them – though I confess to picking up neither the oyster flavour they're supposed to have nor any difference between the two of them. They are undeniably fine though – boil for 15 minutes, slip off the skins in cold water and push them around a pan with cream, parsley, salt, pepper and Parmesan, and be convinced.

VARIETIES: 'Mammoth' and 'Giant' are reliable and delicious varieties of salsify, and 'Russian Giant' or 'Black Giant of Russia', of scorzonera.

STARTING OFF: Sow direct in April at 1cm deep.

POSITION: A sunny position in a well-prepared soil.

SPACING: The seeds are large so it is easy to space them at around 5cm apart, thinning to 15cm as they grow.

PRODUCTIVITY/EFFICIENCY: They will occupy the ground for almost a year, but require little input while they grow.

GROWING: Keep weed free but be careful not to damage roots by hoeing.

POTENTIAL PROBLEMS: Relatively untroubled.

HARVEST: Harvest the roots from October to February. Earth up, or cover with an upturned pot (holes covered), any that you don't eat over winter and the plants will provide you with two or three cuttings of tender green shoots to eat.

SEA KALE

Crambe maritima. Hardy perennial.

A seashore favourite that can be grown in the garden for an early spring harvest when there is little on the menu. The young leaves are pretty good - mild and succulent in salads - but the shoots are incredible, with a flavour like asparagus and the finest hazelnuts. Cover plants as you might rhubarb to force shoots early. The flowers, with their bright honey flavour, shouldn't be overlooked - try them raw in salads.

VARIETIES: You could try the variety 'Lily White' or the larger species C. *cordifolia*.

STARTING OFF: Source plants from a specialist supplier or divide established plants in spring. You can also sow seed in pots in spring, planting out when around 10cm tall, but germination can be very slow.

POSITION: As you might imagine given its origins, it will tolerate most well-drained soils and a certain amount of exposure, and grows well in coastal areas. Prefers neutral and alkaline conditions and full sun, but tolerates some shade.

SPACING: 60cm apart.

PRODUCTIVITY/EFFICIENCY: You can make two or three cuttings of young shoots every year and begin cropping the year after planting out. Shoots, young leaves, flower heads and roots are all edible.

GROWING: Little maintenance required.

POTENTIAL PROBLEMS: Protect from slugs.

HARVEST: Blanch young shoots with a forcer in early spring and cut when a good size. Pick young leaves in spring, flower heads in summer, and dig the roots around the outside of the plant in winter.

SHALLOTS

Allium cepa ascalonicum. Hardy bulb.

I grow more shallots each year, and I suggest you do too: they are expensive to buy, but easy to grow and with such an array of sweet to full-on flavours to choose from. Peeled and used whole in stews, cooked to a soft glossiness in red wine or used as you would onions, shallots really are worth what little trouble they ask of you.

VARIETIES: Try 'Echalotes Grise' for a highly prized, mild gourmet shallot, and 'Longor' and 'Jermor' for delicious and long shallots. 'Red Sun' is round with a reddish-brown skin, or you could try the 'Banana' shallot, which is a cross between an onion and a shallot and combines the best of both.

STARTING OFF: Push sets into the soil in February or March (November/December in milder areas) so the tips are level with or just below the surface. Growing from seed, shallots will make a single bulb in the first year so broadcast sparingly in March or April in wide drills covering with a thin layer of soil.

POSITION: A sunny spot in soil with good drainage.

SPACING: 20cm apart in all directions, if planting in blocks, or 15cm apart and 20cm between rows. For seed-grown shallots thin to 3–4cm.

PRODUCTIVITY/EFFICIENCY: Shallots will occupy the ground for around 4 months.

GROWING: Keep weed free and water in dry weather as bulbs are swelling.

POTENTIAL PROBLEMS: Generally trouble free.

HARVEST: From July, pull the shallots as the leaves begin to yellow. Dry them in the sun for a few days and they should store happily through the winter.

SIBERIAN PEA TREE

Caragana arborescens. Deciduous small tree.

The combination of nitrogen-fixing, soil-enriching qualities, lovely yellow flowers that are adored by the bees and tasty, pea-like pods make the Siberian pea tree a real favourite. The pods have a fine flavour when raw or lightly steamed, but don't let them get too big as they become progressively tougher and lose their charm. The peas can be dried and kept for some time, but they will need soaking overnight and boiling for 20 minutes like other dried pulses.

VARIETIES: You could try *C. arborescens* 'Pendula' for a weeping form or 'Nana' for a more compact version.

STARTING OFF: Source plants from a good supplier or sow seed in pots, potting on until a suitable size for planting out is reached.

POSITION: Full sun and well-drained soil. The Siberian pea tree is happy on poor soils and exposed sites.

SPACING: Reaches 3m high by 2m wide in a UK climate but can reach twice this in a warmer climate.

PRODUCTIVITY/EFFICIENCY: A very productive small tree which begins to fruit in its fourth year, and whose pods and seeds can be eaten fresh or dried for later use.

GROWING: Little maintenance required.

POTENTIAL PROBLEMS: Slugs and snails can be a nuisance to young plants, but once established they are pest and disease free.

HARVEST: Pick young pods in midsummer when around 3cm long. Pods larger than this can be shelled for the peas inside. For peas for storage, harvest pods that have turned brown and allow them to dry further under cover before shelling.

SMALL-LEAVED LIME

Tilia species. Deciduous tree.

After three years, the small-leaved limes I planted not far from a watery ditch that runs through one of the fields here, suddenly became hugely productive. Their thin, delicate leaves, picked small and succulent, provide substance and nutty flavour to salads, especially in spring when the garden is less productive than summer and autumn.

VARIETIES: Small-leaved lime *Tilia cordata* but you could also try *T. platyphyllos*.

STARTING OFF: Source plants from a specialist nursery.

POSITION: Happy on most soils and in sun or shade.

SPACING: If allowed to grow to full size, *Tilia* species can reach 20m tall and 12m wide. Happily, they coppice well and can be kept to around 4m in width.

PRODUCTIVITY/EFFICIENCY: Young leaves are produced from spring until autumn. Leaves are mineral rich and will fertilise the area in which they grow.

GROWING: Coppice at around 6 years old and thereafter every 3 or 4 years.

POTENTIAL PROBLEMS: Generally pest and disease free.

HARVEST: Pick young leaves throughout the growing season.

SOCIETY GARLIC

Tulbaghia violacea. Half-hardy perennial.

This fabulous perennial is my favourite of the society garlics. I don't harvest the long thin leaves and stems; it's the pale pink flowers at their tips that I'm after – they have a full-on flush of garlic flavour but without a hint of harshness. They lose texture and flavour when cooked, so I use them scattered raw in salads and floating in more cocktails than is good for me.

VARIETIES: The named varieties have been bred for their differing ornamental characteristics rather than flavour; however, 'Silver Lace' has larger flowers.

STARTING OFF: Source plants from a good supplier or sow in modules 5cm or so deep, under cover in spring or autumn. Pot on once when the roots are showing and then plant out. You can also divide established plants in autumn.

POSITION: A sunny, sheltered spot with moisture-retentive and well-drained soil. Does well in a pot.

SPACING: 50cm apart.

PRODUCTIVITY/EFFICIENCY: A single plant will give a supply of flowers and leaves from mid-spring into autumn.

GROWING: Protect with a deep mulch over winter in more northerly areas or grow in a tunnel or greenhouse.

POTENTIAL PROBLEMS: Generally pest and disease free.

HARVEST: Pick flowers throughout the summer and autumn.

SOLOMON'S SEAL

Polygonatum species. Hardy perennial.

A well-known plant, largely grown as an ornamental but with delicious early shoots that taste like the very sweetest asparagus. Not the most prolific plant in the garden, but one that loves a damp, shady spot - and there's not much that will give you such a delicious crop from those conditions. Any shoots you don't pick will extend into arches from which beautiful white flowers hang like earrings.

VARIETIES: Most *Polygonatum* species are edible, although *P. commutatum* is the largest of them. Variegated varieties tend to produce less than others.

STARTING OFF: Source plants from a good supplier or divide established plants in spring.

POSITION: A moist but well-drained soil in light or deep shade.

SPACING: 30cm apart.

PRODUCTIVITY/EFFICIENCY: This plant is a slow coloniser and will take some years to establish enough for cropping.

GROWING: Little maintenance required.

POTENTIAL PROBLEMS: Use your chosen slug deterrent on young plants.

HARVEST: Cut shoots at ground level when they are around 25cm tall, leaving the growth that follows to grow on and sustain the plant.

SORREL

Rumex acetosa (Broadleaved), *Rumex scutatus* (Buckler leaved) and *Rumex sanguineus* (Red-veined). Hardy perennial.

With a glorious lemon sharpness, not dissimilar to rhubarb or gooseberries, sorrel is one of my favourite leaves. Picked young and small, the leaves add brightness and zip to mixed leaf salads but are perhaps at their very best thrown into a pan of hot new potatoes with butter and shaken to create the silkiest of sauces. Sorrel is really fine with fish and eggs too.

VARIETIES: Broadleaved with its large leaves is ideal for cooking or try Buckler leaved, which is small and perfect for a salad. You could also try Red-veined sorrel, or pick some from the wild.

STARTING OFF: Sow in spring or autumn in modules under cover or direct, planting out as soon as the roots are showing.

POSITION: Tolerant of most soils. It will run to seed less quickly if given some shade.

SPACING: 30cm apart.

PRODUCTIVITY/EFFICIENCY: You will get a good supply of leaves early and late in the growing season.

GROWING: Water during dry weather to slow running to seed.

POTENTIAL PROBLEMS: Generally untroubled.

HARVEST: Pick or cut leaves as required.

SPINACH

Spinacia oleracea. Hardy annual.

I used to grow vast swathes of spinach. I love its grassy freshness wilted in omelettes, tarts, gratins and uncooked in leafy salads. But I've discovered so many other fabulous spinach-alikes, such as Mexican tree spinach and New Zealand spinach (see pages 63 and 69), which deserve some room that something's had to give. I'd still not be without regular spinach, and if anything, I love it all the more for being one on the spectrum of fine spinachy leaves.

VARIETIES: 'Giant Winter' is good for an autumn sowing as it withstands cold well. Use bolt-resistant varieties such as 'Matador' and 'Medania' for June to August sowings.

STARTING OFF: Sow successively from February to September in modules under cover and plant out once roots are showing. Direct sowings can be made from March.

POSITION: A moisture-retentive soil in part-shade in the hottest months. Spinach will crop happily from an early or late sowing under cover.

SPACING: 5–7cm apart for baby leaves and 15–20cm for larger ones, with 30cm between rows (less for baby leaves).

PRODUCTIVITY/EFFICIENCY: This is a quick-growing crop especially if grown for baby leaves. Plants can regrow after harvesting.

GROWING: Keep soil moist by watering and mulching to prevent bolting.

POTENTIAL PROBLEMS: Very few, though slugs can be a nuisance to young plants and flea beetle similarly so, once in a while.

HARVEST: Cut leaves at 3cm or so above the ground.

SPRING ONIONS

Allium cepa. Hardy bulb.

As with radishes, spring onions are exactly the thing to grow if you're looking for a swift confidence boost. Quick, easy and reliable to get to harvest, their sweet-sharp flavour livens up salads, soups or (even better, if you ask me) griddled to go with pretty much anything.

VARIETIES: 'North Holland Blood Red' and 'White Lisbon' are classic and delicious. 'White Lisbon Winter Hardy' will give you an overwintering crop for early harvest. 'Purplette' forms a round bulb, which can be grown on for pickling if desired.

STARTING OFF: Sow successively outside from February to June and again in August/September for an early spring crop.

POSITION: A sunny well-drained spot but will tolerate some shade.

SPACING: Thin to around 10cm apart.

PRODUCTIVITY/EFFICIENCY: Spring onions take up little space and are ready around 2 months from sowing.

GROWING: Keep weed free and water in dry weather. Protect winter crops in harsh weather.

POTENTIAL PROBLEMS: Use crop rotation to avoid onion downy mildew and white rot.

HARVEST: Pull when around 15cm.

SPROUTING BROCCOLI

Brassica oleracea var. *italica*. Hardy biennial, mostly grown as an annual.

Easy to grow and with a long season of repeated picking, sprouting broccoli is a wonderful cold-weather harvest. Much as I love calabrese in the summer (see page 17), the depth of flavour and nuttiness of sprouting broccoli has me looking forward to the dark months. Slice off the flowering heads, steam and serve with melted butter – better still, with an anchovy or two mashed into it.

VARIETIES: 'Rudolph' is a good early variety, producing from

October to January, or try 'White Eye', 'Red Arrow' or 'Late Purple' for crops from February to April.

STARTING OFF: Sow seed in modules under cover from March to May, planting out in June when 10–15cm high.

POSITION: Full sun in a composted, well-drained but moisture-retentive soil.

SPACING: 60cm apart.

PRODUCTIVITY/EFFICIENCY: Each plant will produce spears over 2–3 months. The later varieties are particularly useful, being harvested during the hungry gap.

GROWING: Keep the soil weed free and moist.

POTENTIAL PROBLEMS: Fleece against pigeons and butterflies. Rotate crops to avoid clubroot and plant deeply (up to first true leaves) to avoid cabbage root fly.

HARVEST: Cut spears when the buds are showing but before they flower. Regular harvesting encourages more spears and plants can be cropped for around 2 months.

SQUASH

Cucurbita species. Half-hardy annual.

A word of advice: admire the gourds, hollow out the pumpkins, and eat only the squash. Better still, be very, very particular about which squash you grow. The best varieties really do sit head and shoulders above the rest of the crowd. As with tomatoes and chillies, grow a few varieties – it will offer you insurance if conditions don't suit one variety, while giving you a range of textures and flavours. Squash is very adaptable in the kitchen –

I love it roasted with garlic, olive oil and rosemary, puréed for puddings, and diced and simmered in stock for pasta sauces.

VARIETIES: A huge variety of colour, shape and texture is available. 'Uchiki Kuri' produces good harvests of sweet, onion-shaped squash. Productive and sweet butternut squash are 'Ponca' and 'Early Butternut'. 'Crown Prince' is my favourite, with its sweet flesh and a duck-egg blue exterior. 'Acorn Table' has a beautiful leaf-shape and produces many incised, dark-green fruits.

STARTING OFF: Sow in 9cm pots in April, with the seeds on their edge vertically rather than laid flat to prevent rotting, and plant out from early June to the end of July.

POSITION: Full sun in a rich, moisture-retentive soil.

SPACING: At least 1m apart. In general, trailing vine types need more space than bush varieties but trailing varieties can thread their way through other crops.

PRODUCTIVITY/EFFICIENCY: Squash will occupy the ground for around 3–4 months, and require little more than watering once in a while.

GROWING: They like moist soil so keep watered in dry weather.

POTENTIAL PROBLEMS: Protect young plants from slugs and snails for the first few weeks.

HARVEST: Cut squash and pumpkins once they sound hollow, leaving a 5cm stalk to prevent rotting. Keep them outside with their undersides upwards in order for them to fully ripen. Bring the squash inside before the first frosts and store somewhere light and cool. Leaves and shoots also edible.

STINGING NETTLES

Urtica dioica. Hardy perennial, mostly grown reluctantly.

If there's one thing most of us grow well, it's nettles. Weeds to most, nutritious greens and a source of nitrogen-rich leaves for making a plant feed to a few. As long as you can keep nettles and your other precious plants apart, there's no reason you can't learn to love them – try young leaves steamed or wilted in place of spinach in tarts especially.

VARIETIES: Needs little introduction and is readily available almost everywhere.

STARTING OFF: If you need to introduce it, start from seed or, easier still, pull up runners and plant where you wish them to grow.

POSITION: Prefers a rich soil but will tolerate most, as well we know.

SPACING: 70–80cm apart.

PRODUCTIVITY/EFFICIENCY: Provides nutritious greens when little else is around. It is also a mineral accumulator, drawing up many nutrients from deep in the soil, making a great liquid feed or mulch.

GROWING: Cut back flowering stems to check spreading and also to promote fresh young growth.

POTENTIAL PROBLEMS: Generally pest and disease free.

HARVEST: Wearing gloves, pick the young tips in spring.

SWEDE

Brassica napus var. *napobrassica*. Hardy biennial, mostly grown as an annual.

One day, very shortly if I have anything to do with it, there will be a revival in swedes' fortunes. As with turnips, most of us see these spherical roots as livestock feed, when, with good varieties and care in the kitchen, they are every bit the equal of squash. Steamed or boiled until just cooked, mashed and over-peppered they make a fine side, as well as a sweet-savoury root in all manner of stews and gratins. Try a short row and I promise you'll expand it next year.

VARIETIES: 'Ruby', 'Willemsburger' and 'Helenor' are all good.

STARTING OFF: Sow direct from May to early June. Earlier sowings can be made in February under protection.

POSITION: Full sun in moisture-retentive and well-drained soil.

SPACING: Space rows 35cm apart and thin to around 20cm. If block planting, space maincrops 30cm apart in all directions and early ones at half that.

PRODUCTIVITY/EFFICIENCY: Maincrop swedes are in the ground for around 6 months and can be eaten up to December, after which they risk becoming woody.

GROWING: Keep soil moist but don't water too heavily at once after a dry spell as the roots can split.

POTENTIAL PROBLEMS: Fleece against flea beetle. Control slugs to prevent them eating swede tops as this can encourage rotting.

HARVEST: Begin harvesting when roots are the size you want them. Harvest as needed.

SWEETCORN

Zea mays. Half-hardy annual.

Barbecued sweetcorn, fresh from the plant, smothered in butter, lime juice and too much pepper and salt is about as good as summer outdoor eating gets. They are easy to grow but a little hit and miss, needing a long hot summer to thrive. Take care with varieties – there are plenty of very sweet ones, but I prefer the ones with a balance of wider flavours.

VARIETIES: 'Sweet Nugget' and 'Sweetie' are among the sweetest varieties. 'Golden Bantam' and 'Stowell's Evergreen' have a good balance of flavour and sweetness, the latter being a very old variety that will stay ripe on the plant for a long time. You could also try 'Minipop' for baby sweetcorn or 'Strawberry' for your own popcorn.

STARTING OFF: Sow in 9cm pots in April under cover and plant out as soon as the last frosts have passed. Sow direct from May to June. Sweetcorn can be grown under cover and baby sweetcorn works well in pots.

POSITION: Warm and sheltered in a composted, moisture-retentive and well-draining soil.

SPACING: 15–30cm apart, depending on variety, but do plant in blocks rather than rows as this makes wind pollination more effective. Make sure you leave at least 8m between super-sweet and non-super-sweet varieties, or you may find that cross-pollination makes the super-sweet less so.

PRODUCTIVITY/EFFICIENCY: Sweetcorn will occupy the ground for 8–20 weeks. You will get around 8 mini-cobs per plant and

2–3 large ones, with harvests possible from August to October with the right varieties.

GROWING: Growing courgettes and squash around your sweetcorn will help keep it weed free. Grow in blocks rather than rows, as sweetcorn is wind pollinated and success rates are improved. Provide support if growing on an exposed site.

POTENTIAL PROBLEMS: Sow in pots and transplant if you have mice and bird problems.

HARVEST: Larger cobs are ready when the tassels turn brown and the juices are milky when you push the cob with your thumbnail. Pick baby sweetcorn when around 7cm long.

SWEET PEPPERS

Capsicum annuum. Half-hardy annual.

I have to admit, I rarely grow sweet peppers – I'm loath to give up any of the undercover space that chillies could take, and I prefer the sweet, mild chillies such as 'Apricot', 'Padron' and 'Poblano' to sweet peppers. That said, if you like them, they aren't tricky to grow, but they are particular. Choose good varieties, start them early, give them heat and light throughout their lives and feed them often and you'll be rewarded in all but the coolest summers.

VARIETIES: 'California Wonder' for a traditional bell shape, 'Marconi Rosso' and 'Jimmy Nardello' are long, red and sweet. 'Hamik' is possibly the sweetest of all and 'Tequila' is early ripening and purple.

STARTING OFF: Sow in modules in a propagator or airing cupboard in February/March (no later than April), potting on into

9cm pots and then again as soon as the roots show through the holes in the bottom. It should be warm enough to plant in a tunnel or greenhouse by the end of April. Germination is usually slow.

POSITION: For best results grow in a tunnel or greenhouse.

SPACING: 45–60cm apart, depending on variety, although they are also happy grown in pots.

PRODUCTIVITY/EFFICIENCY: Yields vary greatly between varieties but you should be able to pick peppers from midsummer to early autumn.

GROWING: A weekly comfrey feed is essential if growing in pots.

POTENTIAL PROBLEMS: Rarely affected by pests and diseases.

HARVEST: Harvest from green through to red when they will be at their sweetest.

SWEET POTATO

Ipomoea batatas. Half-hardy perennial climber.

Slowly, these tropical/sub-tropical favourites have been selected and bred to stand more than a racing chance in our cool climate, and you can now expect to get a good harvest in a sunny location. Unlike more familiar potatoes, sweet potatoes grow as a trailing, scrambling vine that can cover 1–2m but it won't climb even if you give them a structure to ascend. I like them best mashed, roasted and as chips.

VARIETIES: 'Georgia Jet' is very reliable in the UK climate or try 'Beauregard Improved' or 'Henry', which with its compact habit is very good for containers.

STARTING OFF: Source slips (unrooted cuttings) of named varieties from a good supplier. The slips may look wilted when they arrive but are easily revived by putting in water overnight. Pot them up so that the stem is in compost right up to the first leaves and then put them in an unheated propagator or cover the pot with a clear plastic bag until they have rooted. Plant sweet potatoes out after all danger of frost has passed. They grow best in temperatures of 21–25°C and are very happy in a polytunnel or greenhouse. If growing outside, warm the ground with black polythene some weeks before planting and plant through the polythene. Covering with a fleece or a cloche will help them grow.

POSITION: Fertile, humus-rich and well-drained soil in a sunny sheltered spot.

SPACING: 30cm apart along the rows with 70cm between each row.

PRODUCTIVITY/EFFICIENCY: Sweet potatoes will occupy the ground for 4–5 months.

GROWING: Plants growing under cover will be more vigorous and support may be needed. Feed plants in containers every couple of weeks with a liquid seaweed or comfrey feed.

POTENTIAL PROBLEMS: Generally pest and disease free but can be a risk in cooler parts of the UK.

HARVEST: Tubers are ready when the foliage starts to turn yellow in late summer/early autumn. For larger tubers, leave in the ground for as long as possible but dig them up before the frosts arrive. If the sweet potatoes are for storing then leave to dry in the sun for a couple of hours after digging and then cure further in a greenhouse or polytunnel for around 10 days. Store somewhere cool and dry after this.

TOMATILLOS

Physalis ixocarpa and *P. philadelphica*. Half-hardy annual.

Mexican in origin, tomatillos unsurprisingly take perfectly to the salsas and sauces that characterise that fine, fresh cuisine. Similar to tomatoes in habit and appearance, the flavour of tomatillos is on the fence between sweet and citrus, and once you get your mind past the expectation that it should be sweet like a tomato, they really are very good in the kitchen. And it's hard not to love something that comes in its own papery wrapper.

VARIETIES: Try 'Dr Wyche's Yellow', 'Tomatillo Verde' and 'Tomatillo Purple'.

STARTING OFF: Sow in modules on a window sill, or in an airing cupboard or heated propagator 6–8 weeks before the last frosts, potting on once when the roots are showing at the bottom of the module.

POSITION: Sunny and warm with a rich well-drained soil.

SPACING: Allow around 60cm apart in all directions if providing support, and double that if allowing them to sprawl on the soil (they may produce more fruit this way).

PRODUCTIVITY/EFFICIENCY: Tomatillos are prolific and can produce 10kg of fruit per plant.

GROWING: Tie in the tomatillos as they grow if you are using support.

POTENTIAL PROBLEMS: Very few.

HARVEST: Harvest when the papery cases split open. Fruits are produced from July to October.

TOMATOES

Lycopersicon esculentum. Half-hardy annual.

It is absolutely compulsory to grow 'Sungold' tomatoes at least once in your life. Although it may be something that brings you considerable unhappiness: every shop-bought tomato will disappoint from that day forward. Their blend of sweet and sharp with a juiciness and fine texture is hard to match. I'd suggest growing tomatoes in all three main sizes. Let flavour be your guide. I always grow a few different varieties each year, for different flavours, sizes and textures, trying at least two new varieties in the hope of finding a new favourite.

VARIETIES: An enormous variety is available to you ranging from white through yellow, orange and red to black, and from the size of a currant to as big as your hand. 'Sungold' and 'Honeycomb' as cherry tomatoes, 'Black Krim' or 'Shimmer' as medium-sized tomatoes, and 'Costoluto Fiorentino' and 'Big Brandywine' as fine hand-filling fruit.

STARTING OFF: Sow in modules in February or March and put on a window sill or in an airing cupboard or propagator. Pot on when the roots are showing. Plant out when the flowers are just opening on the first truss, making sure this is after the last frost if growing your tomatoes outside.

POSITION: As much sun and warmth as you can give them and in a composted soil with good drainage.

SPACING: 45–60cm apart, depending on variety.

PRODUCTIVITY/EFFICIENCY: Tomatoes will supply you with a steady stream of fruit from June/July to October.

GROWING: Indeterminate varieties (those that grow high) require support as the main stem grows. Growing tips should be pinched out when the plant reaches the height you want it. For outdoor-grown indeterminate varieties, pinch out the growing tip when there are 4 or 5 trusses of fruit to encourage ripening. For those growing under cover, most people pinch out when there are 7 or 8 trusses. Pull off the lower leaves to the next fruiting truss to keep airflow good. Bush varieties won't need pinching out at all. Pinch out the shoots that grow between the stem and the side branches – this helps direct the plant's energies to the fruit, rather than unnecessary green growth. Water regularly, making sure it is the soil or compost that gets wet, not the plant – wet leaves and fruit encourages disease. Once the plant flowers, feed every fortnight with a high potassium feed.

POTENTIAL PROBLEMS: Blight is your main worry. Water at the base to minimise blight problems and don't overwater as this can reduce the flavour. Grow basil around your tomatoes to deter whitefly.

HARVEST: Pick cherry tomatoes a little under-ripe as they can split when fully ripe. Other varieties should be picked as soon as they have reached the colour appropriate to the variety. As cold weather approaches, pick your last tomatoes green. They will ripen in the warmth inside.

TURNIPS

Brassica rapa. Hardy biennial, mostly grown as an annual.

Before you consign turnips (along with swede, see page 102) to the pigeonhole labelled 'livestock feed', try the varieties below. When you get them to the kitchen, roast them with honey, or dice them small to take the place of the rice in a risotto where they'll soak up the flavours from the stock and herbs. The leaves are really tasty too – a nutty, yet sweet brassica flavour that makes a fine pasta sauce when wilted in olive oil.

VARIETIES: 'Snowball Early White' will give you sweet globe-shaped turnips through summer and into autumn. 'Noir d'Hiver' is a black-skinned performer in cold weather or try 'Purple Top Milan' for purple-flushed baby turnips.

STARTING OFF: Sow quick-maturing varieties direct every 2–3 weeks, from March to July. Sow maincrops direct in July and August.

POSITION: Moisture-retentive and well-drained soil in sun or part-shade.

SPACING: Space quick-maturing varieties 15cm apart in all directions in blocks and 22cm in all directions for maincrops.

PRODUCTIVITY/EFFICIENCY: Quick-maturing varieties can be ready in 5 weeks and are great for catch-cropping. Maincrops can occupy the ground from July until New Year, or longer if you harvest their leaves.

GROWING: Water in hot dry weather to prevent splitting or bolting.

POTENTIAL PROBLEMS: Fleece against flea beetle, cabbage root fly, pigeons and butterflies.

HARVEST: Pull quick-maturing varieties when around 5cm in diameter and maincrops when they are around 10cm.

VIOLA 'HEARTSEASE'

Viola tricolor. Also known as: wild pansy and heartsease. Hardy annual.

This one's a bit of a no-brainer. Unless absolutely every square centimetre of soil is covered, you've room for a few viola scattered around the garden or in pots. They'll bring in insects for pollination and to keep the balance of pests-to-beneficial-insects in your favour and, as well as being beautiful, they're delicious and productive. Their flavour, while not mouth-slappingly heavy, is gently sweet and mildly peppery – really good as a little garden nibble or in salads and floating in cocktails.

VARIETIES: None available.

STARTING OFF: Sow in modules in March and again in September, planting out when the roots are showing.

POSITION: Will tolerate some shade and most well-drained soils.

SPACING: 15cm apart.

PRODUCTIVITY/EFFICIENCY: Plants will keep producing flowers for around 5 months, so 2 sowings should give you nearly year-round flowers.

GROWING: Little attention needed.

POTENTIAL PROBLEMS: Few problems.

HARVEST: Pick flower heads as desired.

YACON

Polymnia edulis. Half-hardy perennial.

A fabulous South American tuber that I grow every year: lush, tall, leafy growth is occasionally topped (in the hottest of summers) by small, gorgeous yellow flowers. Underneath this distracting loveliness, tubers are developing. Often swelling disconcertingly late in the season, the tubers come in two sorts: the large ones for eating and the smaller ones to be stored with a little of their growing tip (where next year's shoots emerge) for replanting next year. Buy it once and you have it for life. Their glassy texture is similar to water chestnuts and they are similarly good in stir-fries, but do try them fresh after a day or two of them sweetening in the sun - their flavour is pears crossed with the earliest sharp apples.

VARIETIES: No named varieties although tubers can be yellow, pink, purple, orange or white.

STARTING OFF: Source tubers from a good supplier and plant in damp compost under cover, planting out after the last frosts. You can also split the crown of established plants in spring, ensuring that each section has some root attached.

POSITION: Somewhere sunny and hot in fertile well-drained soil. They are hardy to –5°C.

SPACING: 50cm apart.

PRODUCTIVITY/EFFICIENCY: Yields vary, but expect a typical haul of around six large tubers per plant, though you may get double that.

GROWING: Little required. If leaving in open ground over winter give a thick mulch of compost or straw.

POTENTIAL PROBLEMS: Generally problem free.

HARVEST: Dig the tubers in autumn before the first frosts and store somewhere cool and dark.

WHAT TO GROW

FRUIT AND NUTS

ALMONDS

Prunus dulcis. Deciduous tree.

I've planted a fair few almonds of various varieties and they are particular – sunshine and shelter are a must if you want nuts. The more you dilute this, the less likely you are to have anything to harvest. Spring is their pinch point: get the blossom past the frosts and there's little in your way. Growing your own not only gives you really delicious almonds, but also the prospect of green almonds picked in summer, tasting of fresh peas as much as almonds. Shelled, fresh, home-grown almonds are a rare treat, and a fine beer-snack when pushed around a pan, salted, spiced and honeyed.

VARIETIES: 'Mandaline' and 'Ferragnes' are two relatively recent French varieties, which flower a little later than most, but for the greatest likelihood of success in the majority of this country I'd recommend almond/peach hybrids such as 'Ingrid' and 'Robijn' – they taste as you'd hope a superb almond would, and are hardier and earlier producing than traditional varieties. Check with your supplier to see if your chosen variety needs a pollinator.

STARTING OFF: Buy as a plant or graft your own on to 'St Julien A' or 'Myran' rootstocks.

POSITION: A sunny, sheltered spot with a moisture-retentive but well-drained soil.

SPACING: This varies with rootstock and soil type, but 6m apart is a good rule of thumb.

PRODUCTIVITY/EFFICIENCY: Almonds are self-fertile but will give you more nuts if you grow two or more varieties. Not reliable producers every year but can be heavy yielding.

GROWING: A liquid feed and/or compost/manure mulch around the base will greatly invigorate the plant and boost health and the likelihood of a harvest.

POTENTIAL PROBLEMS: Leaf curl can be a problem so protect leaves from spring rains (which bring the fungus) with a cover if possible but leave access underneath for pollinators. Almond/peach hybrids are less susceptible to leaf curl. Almonds can flower before any pollinators are around, so use a soft paintbrush to do the job yourself. Don't plant almonds near peaches as they can cross-pollinate, resulting in bitter nuts. Protect leaves of young trees from slugs and snails.

HARVEST: In October when the green hull has split and a gentle shake of the tree causes the nuts to drop to the ground, spreading a blanket beneath the tree will ensure that you don't lose any in the grass. The nuts in the centre of the tree may take a few more days to ripen.

ALPINE STRAWBERRIES

Fragaria vesca. Hardy perennial.

If you're looking for a brilliant way of lining a path or bed, you could do far worse than alpine strawberries. As well as providing intensely flavoured berries for year after year, the plants hold their shape over winter, providing low structure to the garden - and as soon as the days lengthen and there's a whiff of heat in the air, the fruit pop out. Not the sort of thing to feed the five thousand, but perfect as garden treats or allowed to dissolve in a glass of fizz.

VARIETIES: 'Mignonette' is the finest red you can grow, or try 'Yellow Wonder' or 'Pineapple Crush' for creamy yellow strawberries, which birds won't bother with quite so much.

STARTING OFF: Alpine strawberry seed is very small so it is easiest sown in trays. A February sowing under cover will give you fruit in the same year. Leave the seed on the surface and put the tray inside a plastic bag to prevent the soil drying out, and uncover as soon as germination starts. When big enough to handle, prick seedlings out into modules or small pots, planting out when the roots are showing. Sowings can be made direct from April – cover the seed with just a dusting of compost.

POSITION: Tolerant of most soils and in full sun or some shade.

SPACING: 15–30cm apart.

PRODUCTIVITY/EFFICIENCY: You will get a steady supply of alpine strawberries from May to September. They are also happy growing in containers.

GROWING: Keep watered whilst establishing. An occasional mulch of compost will give you greater yields. A fortnightly feed with comfrey tea whilst flowering will encourage yet more flowers and fruit.

POTENTIAL PROBLEMS: Relatively untroubled by pests and disease.

HARVEST: Pick when deep red (white/yellow varieties when soft to the touch) every day or two from May until September.

A

APPLES

Malus domestica. Deciduous tree.

There are so many choices when it comes to apples - flavour, aroma, texture, size of tree, season of eating - that you need to sit yourself down and ask yourself some serious questions before deciding. First of all, do you have room for more than one tree? If not, the vast selection becomes considerably narrowed to one of the few self-fertile varieties - 'Braeburn' or 'Sunset' for example. One of the biggest distinctions to be aware of is between early and later apples: as a rule, the earlier in season an apple is ready to pick, the less time it stores for. 'Beauty of Bath' will give you perhaps six days in August to eat it once it's left the tree, whereas an 'Adam's Pearmain' picked in October will give you six months. It's not just about storing qualities though - you'll not find the earlies in the shops for precisely the reason that they don't store, so you open up different flavours and an early part of the season if you grow them yourself. There's no right or wrongs, just what you prefer.

VARIETIES: There are varieties for eating, cooking, juicing and cider, with some of them (such as 'Veitches Perfection') suitable for more than one of these purposes.

Apples are grafted on to a rootstock, which determines the ultimate size of tree. Several rootstocks are available, including MM26 is dwarfing, MM106 semi-dwarfing, and rootstocks M25 and MM111 will make trees over 5m tall. For good pollination the trees you choose must have compatible flowering times or be self-fertile. Check with your supplier to see if your chosen variety needs a pollinator.

'Orleans Reinette', 'Old Somerset Russet', 'Lord Lambourne' and 'Ashmead's Kernel' are delicious eaters. Try 'Annie

Elizabeth' or 'Bramley's Seedling' for cookers. 'Kingston Black', 'Dabinett' and 'Brown's Apple' are very good cider apples, or try 'Veitch's Perfection' for a lovely cooker and eater.

STARTING OFF: Source grafted trees as maidens or 2–3-year-old bushes and trees.

POSITION: Rootstocks are tolerant of most soils, but MM111 and MM106 are better for heavy clay and wetter soils. A sunny spot is important for sweet apples, especially late ripening ones, although cooking apples will ripen sufficiently in some shade. Fruit set will be better with shelter from the worst of the winds.

SPACING: 2.5–9m apart, depending on rootstock.

PRODUCTIVITY/EFFICIENCY: Carefully chosen varieties can give you eating and cooking apples from late July through to March. While trained varieties such as stepovers, cordons and espaliers give you less fruit, they can be grown in spaces that otherwise wouldn't be used, e.g. along the edge of a path.

GROWING: Water in dry weather, especially in the first year and as often as required if growing in a pot. Underplant with comfrey, which is high in nitrogen and potassium, cutting it to the ground a couple of times a year and allowing the leaves to rot down. Prune bushes and trees in winter, and trained varieties in summer.

POTENTIAL PROBLEMS: Use pheromone traps if codling moth is a problem. Some varieties (such as 'Lord Derby' and 'Ellison's Orange') are resistant to scab and canker. If your tree is affected with scab, prune blistered stems and incinerate along with any leaves and fruit affected by the tell-tale blotches. For canker, remove all affected stems, cut out any affected wood on large branches and paint wounds with a wound paint.

HARVEST: In general, the later the apple ripens the longer it will store for, with earlier ripening apples best eaten within a week or so of picking. When ripe the apple should come away easily if you lift gently and give a quarter turn. Leave for longer if not.

APRICOTS

Prunus armeniaca. Deciduous tree.

A home-grown apricot is a fine thing – it may not have the shoe-splattering juiciness of a peach perhaps, but it has a depth of flavour and richness which comes only with apricots that are separated from the tree when absolutely at their ripe peak. They need sun and shelter to be at their best.

VARIETIES: 'Flavourcot'® and 'Tomcot' are delicious, or try 'Moorpark' for a later variety. Try an older variety such as 'Bredase', or 'Aprigold' for a dwarf variety. Self-fertile.

STARTING OFF: Source grafted trees as maidens, 2- and 3-year-old bushes, or as trained forms.

POSITION: Sunny and sheltered in a deep soil that is moisture retentive and with good drainage.

SPACING: Depending on type of rootstock, space up to 4.5m apart.

PRODUCTIVITY/EFFICIENCY: Mature fan-trained trees can give up to 14kg of fruit, and a tree up to 55kg, which is a pretty heavy harvest of a fruit that is usually expensive to buy. Apricots can begin to produce in their second year.

GROWING: Thin fruits if crowded to allow remaining ones to get to a larger size. Give an annual feed of compost of cut comfrey.

Cut out diseased and dead wood during the growing season between May and September.

POTENTIAL PROBLEMS: Choose later-flowering varieties to avoid late frosts damaging apricot flowers, or plant against a sunny, south-facing wall. Newer varieties (such as 'Flavourcot'®) are less susceptible to bacterial canker. Pruning in midsummer helps minimise the risk of bacterial canker and silver leaf: any affected areas should be cut out and incinerated.

HARVEST: Between July and September. Pick when fruits are just tender, aromatic and when they separate easily from the tree with only the slightest persuasion.

ASIAN PEARS

Pyrus species. Also known as: apple pears or Chinese pears. Deciduous tree.

There are a few species that come under the Asian pear umbrella, but *Pyrus pyrifolia* is the one for the delicious fruit. Despite the name and a pear-like flavour, the fruit resembles a lightly russeted apple sprayed gold, yet is altogether juicier and more crisp than the familiar apple. Very popular in parts of the Middle and Far East (Korea especially), they will grow perfectly well in the UK - I'm mystified as to why they are so uncommon here. Pick early and crisp, and allow some to ripen further to become honeyed and more juicy.

VARIETIES: Try 'Shinsui' for an early Asian pear and 'Shinko' for a later one. 'Shin Li' has a hint of cinnamon. Asian pears are not self-fertile so you will need another variety with a compatible flowering time.

STARTING OFF: Source grafted maidens or 2-year-old trees.

POSITION: Full sun in most soils, with good drainage.

SPACING: Up to 9m apart, depending on rootstock used.

PRODUCTIVITY/EFFICIENCY: With careful choice of variety you can have Asian pears from July to October. Trees begin to produce fruit in years 2 or 3 with 180kg of fruit possible from a mature tree.

GROWING: Prune every 1–3 years to stimulate new growth. Thin fruit if the young crop is heavy, as allowing too heavy a crop to develop can lead to biennial cropping. Asian pears can be trained as espaliers.

POTENTIAL PROBLEMS: Some varieties of Asian pear are less susceptible to fireblight and bacterial canker.

HARVEST: Leave to ripen fully on the tree as they won't ripen further after picking. They'll leave the tree easily when ready.

AUTUMN OLIVE

Elaeagnus umbellata. Also known as: Japanese silver-berry. Deciduous shrub.

If you have a little space, this is one of the best plants you can grow. Fruitful, fast growing, nitrogen fixing and in leaf for most of the year, autumn olive feeds you and your garden equally. With leaves very similar to the olive, it catches the light beautifully and its abundant intense pink berries are a great late autumn harvest: lightly speckled and a pinker version of redcurrants to the eye, their sharp, full flavour is superb in tarts, preserves and ice creams.

VARIETIES: Try varieties 'Brilliant Rose', 'Big Red' or 'Jewel'. Self-fertile.

STARTING OFF: Source named varieties from suppliers. If growing from seed, sow in trays or modules in autumn and allow the cold to get to it. Pot on once large enough to handle, planting out when filling a 1 litre pot.

POSITION: Tolerant of most situations and soils, including some shade and exposure.

SPACING: Every 2.5m apart for hedging and 5m for individual plants.

PRODUCTIVITY/EFFICIENCY: A heavy-cropping plant, much loved by bees.

GROWING: Prune as necessary to maintain the size you want, bearing in mind it can easily reach 5m or more in height if allowed to.

POTENTIAL PROBLEMS: Generally trouble free.

HARVEST: Run your fingers down the stem to pull fruit into a waiting bag. Berries can be astringent if not fully ripe – I like them when they are still tart but not to the point of wincing; it's very much up to you and your taste buds how early or late you harvest.

BLACKBERRIES

Rubus fruticosus. Deciduous shrub.

As plentiful as blackberries are in urban hedges and rough ground as they are in rural areas, it is very much worth considering them for your garden, as garden varieties tend to be sweeter and more productive than wild blackberries. With the right varieties, you can extend the season from midsummer through well into autumn too. I don't prefer their flavour to wild blackberries – I like the sharpness and occasion of foraging for them – but in many ways I consider them as a separate fruit altogether.

VARIETIES: Growing a range of varieties will keep you in blackberries from July to the first frosts. Try early and vigorous 'Bedford Giant', compact and thornless 'Waldo', or vigorous and later ripening 'Chester Thornless'. Self-fertile.

STARTING OFF: Source named varieties from a supplier. New plants are easily made when shoot tips touch the soil.

POSITION: Tolerant of most soils and in full sun for best fruit.

SPACING: 2.5–3.5m apart, further if allowing the plant to ramble.

PRODUCTIVITY/EFFICIENCY: Heavy crops can be had from July to October from a relatively small space.

GROWING: Allow plant to ramble, or train along horizontal wires.

POTENTIAL PROBLEMS: Net against birds.

HARVEST: Ripe fruit will separate easily from the plant.

BLACKCURRANTS

Ribes nigrum. Deciduous shrub.

One of the must-have fruits, for its leaves as much as the currants. Blackcurrants are pretty indestructible, easy to grow, need minimal maintenance and give such a fine return on your investment for years. Better still, their flavour is way superior to bought currants because you can wait until they are perfectly ripe to pick them, rather than have to harvest them early and firm to withstand the journey to the shelves. The leaves too are one of my favourite flavours of the year – pick a few for fruit tea (honestly, it's one of the few that really are worth it), or for making the very finest sorbet there is.

VARIETIES: Any of the 'Ben' varieties are delicious as well as having good disease resistance with 'Big Ben' having very big berries. 'Titania' is an early variety with a lovely sweet/sharp balance. Self-fertile.

STARTING OFF: Source plants from a good supplier or propagate your own from hardwood cuttings in winter. When planting (in the winter for bare root; any time for potted plants) cut all back almost to the ground and just above a bud.

POSITION: Tolerant of most soils with reasonable drainage but needs full sun.

SPACING: 1.5–2m apart.

PRODUCTIVITY/EFFICIENCY: Cropping starts after 2 years with full cropping at 4 years and they will be productive for 15 or 20 years. With careful choice of cultivars you can have blackcurrants from July to September and each plant can produce around 4kg of fruit.

GROWING: Blackcurrants are hungry and thirsty so give an annual mulch with compost or manure, watering in dry weather whilst fruits are swelling. Prune out one-third of older stems each winter.

POTENTIAL PROBLEMS: Net against birds, particularly in a dry summer. Spray off aphids with a jet of water. Cut off and burn any stems affected with big bud mite, which in turn should help avoid reversion disease.

HARVEST: Blackcurrants are ripe a little while after the berries have turned a deep colour.

BLUE BEAN

Decaisnea fargesii. Also known as: blue sausage fruit and dead man's fingers. Hardy deciduous shrub.

One of my favourite-looking plants: imagine electric blue broad beans hanging from a large-leaved ash and you'll be on the right lines. The pulp inside the pods is the edible bit, tasting delicately of melon. Also within the pods, a clutch of large seeds that fly rather well when spat. Mine have only recently started fruiting, so I'm still at the 'eating them by the plant as they ripen' stage, but I suspect the pulp will be very good in cocktails and fruit salads.

VARIETIES: No named varieties. Self-fertile.

STARTING OFF: I'd start with a plant as they can take a while to get established, though they can be started from seed. Best sown from fresh, ripe seed in autumn in seed trays in a greenhouse or polytunnel. They should germinate in spring after exposure to the temperature fluctuations (stratification) of winter.

POSITION: Sunny or partial shade, and sheltered from cold winds. Moist but well-drained soil.

SPACING: 4m apart.

PRODUCTIVITY/EFFICIENCY: Easy but not highly productive. Self-fertile.

GROWING: An annual mulch will be appreciated.

POTENTIAL PROBLEMS: Very cold hardy, to about −28°C, but flowers and new growth can be damaged by late frosts.

HARVEST: Plants usually start fruiting when 3–4 years old. The pods are picked when blue and soft. Split them open as you would a runner bean and scoop out the flesh with a spoon. Blue beans don't store for very long so enjoy freely when fresh.

BLUEBERRIES

Vaccinium corymbosum. Deciduous shrub.

One of the fruits that almost everyone who grows it, grows in containers. Blueberries need very acidic soil to thrive and the easiest way to ensure they get it is to plant them in a container full of ericaceous compost. The fruit is delicious – many of the varieties available to grow at home have a more intense flavour than those in the shops where they are expensive to buy, yet easy to grow. I've had best success when growing three or so varieties together where good pollination leads to a bumper harvest.

VARIETIES: *V. corymbosum* 'Atlantic' is a vigorous plant producing in July, 'Bluecrop' for large berries in early to mid-August, and 'Chandler' for large sweet berries in late August and September. Blueberries are partially self-fertile meaning that a single plant will produce fruit, but you will get significantly more fruit if you have two or more plants.

STARTING OFF: Source named varieties from a good supplier. Plants are easily propagated by hardwood cuttings.

POSITION: Full sun in a soil with a pH between 4 and 5.5, and that is damp but not waterlogged. They will happily grow in large pots using ericaceous compost.

SPACING: 1.5m apart, or 60cm in a container.

PRODUCTIVITY/EFFICIENCY: Berries ripen over a long time and the right cultivars can supply you with a steady stream of berries from July to September. Although blueberries produce early in their life, they often slowly increase in productivity until cropping fully after 6 years.

GROWING: Mulch generously each year with bark chippings, pine needles or ericaceous compost. Water with rainwater as tap water tends to be too alkaline. Prune out dead, weak and crossing branches as well as growth more than 4 years old to stimulate younger fruit-bearing growth.

POTENTIAL PROBLEMS: Generally problem free, but net against birds.

HARVEST: Pick fruits when they are soft and fully indigo blue.

BLUE HONEYSUCKLE

Lonicera caerulea. Also known as: honeyberry. Hardy deciduous shrub.

Not a climbing plant, as the name suggests it might be, but hardy, prolific in good years and fruiting very early in the season (often in May), blue honeysuckle is one of my favourites. The berries are like stretched blueberries to look at, with a good deep, honeyed (hence the name) edge to their flavour.

VARIETIES: 'Kamchatka' is particularly hardy, or you could try

'Blue Velvet' or 'Mailon' for very large fruits. You will need two different varieties for pollination.

STARTING OFF: Source plants of named varieties from a good supplier or propagate from hardwood cuttings in winter.

POSITION: Tolerant of most soils and in full sun for good fruiting.

SPACING: 1.5m apart.

PRODUCTIVITY/EFFICIENCY: Blue honeysuckles can start producing fruit in their second year and the berries ripen over several weeks. Low maintenance and fruiting when little else is. A good early bee plant too.

GROWING: An occasional mulch with compost would be appreciated.

POTENTIAL PROBLEMS: Generally pest and disease free.

HARVEST: Pick fruit when a dark purple and the fruits have softened.

BOYSENBERRIES

Rubus hybrid. Deciduous shrub.

Supposedly a rather complex cross of blackberry, raspberry, dewberry and loganberry, you might expect (as I did) that boysenberries would have something of an indistinct flavour: nothing of the sort. This is one of the best flavours of the summer – full, fruity, deep and winey. The fruit look a little like long blackberries and are grown in exactly the same way, either in a low-maintenance scramble or trained into a fan.

VARIETIES: No named varieties although some strains are thornless. Self-fertile.

STARTING OFF: Source bare-root plants from a good supplier.

POSITION: A sunny spot. They are tolerant of most soils except very heavy clay and are drought tolerant too.

SPACING: 2m apart.

PRODUCTIVITY/EFFICIENCY: Boysenberries are vigorous growers with heavy crops of berries.

GROWING: An occasional mulch of compost or manure.

POTENTIAL PROBLEMS: Generally pest and disease free.

HARVEST: Pick berries when a deep black colour and they come away easily from the core.

CAPE GOOSEBERRIES

Physalis peruviana. Also known as: Inca berry, Aztec berry, giant ground cherry and golden berry. Half-hardy perennial, often grown as an annual.

I've probably turned my nose up at a hundred or more of these fruits, wrapped in their papery nest – removed from the sides of cheesecakes, tarts and ice creams served at the end of pub meals of varying quality. The fruit look and taste like a golden cross between a cherry tomato and a regular gooseberry. I've not had a good one but in the spirit of adventure, this year I'm going to grow plenty and try them in all sorts of recipes that sit in that sweet/sharp territory they inhabit, and see if I can't make friends with them, as I have with its close relative, the tomatillo.

VARIETIES: The dwarf 'Pineapple' is one of the few named varieties available.

STARTING OFF: Sow seeds in modules under cover in February and March, and pot on when the roots are showing. Plant out after last frosts or grow under cover.

POSITION: Tolerant of most soils but likes reasonable drainage. It can be grown as a perennial if sheltered from frosts.

SPACING: 60cm apart.

PRODUCTIVITY/EFFICIENCY: Cape gooseberries are heavy yielding with very little input.

GROWING: Lightly spray plants with water or tap the stems to encourage pollination. Ensure soil stays moist. Stake plants as necessary. Plants will produce more fruit and less leaf if not fed.

POTENTIAL PROBLEMS: Generally pest and disease free.

HARVEST: Collect fruit that has dropped to the ground. They are ready to eat when the fruit inside the papery husk has turned a golden yellow, which may happen a while after they have dropped. They can store for over a month if left in their husks.

CHERRIES

Prunus avium and *Prunus cerasus*. Deciduous tree.

There are some days in midsummer when there's nothing I'd rather eat than cherries. Straight from the tree, on pizza, in salads or clafoutis, they are part of almost every meal. I grow a few different varieties and I love them all, but they can be an expensive (and heartbreaking) way of growing bird food. You can load the odds in your favour by growing them trained against a wall (easy to net) or as dwarf varieties within a fruit cage, or try the white varieties, which the birds are less interested in.

VARIETIES: So many lovely sweet varieties – 'Stella', 'Summit' or 'Kordia' among them, along with 'Vega' if you are interested in trying a white cherry. Try 'Morello' for a sour cherry or a 'Duke' type such as 'May Duke' if you fancy a cross between a sweet and sour cherry. Check with your supplier if your chosen variety requires a pollinator.

STARTING OFF: Easy and cheap bought as young plants, or graft your own on to a rootstock. Cherries can be bought partially trained if you are planning to fan train.

POSITION: Deep, fertile and well-drained soil. Full sun for sweet cherries, although 'Morello' needs less heat and will happily produce where little else will when planted against a north- or east-facing wall.

SPACING: Depends entirely on the rootstock you choose, but in general allow between 3–4m if using a Gisela rootstock, and 4.5–5m for a Colt rootstock. If you only have room for one then check that your chosen variety is self-fertile. If planting more than one then ensure that pollination groups are compatible.

PRODUCTIVITY/EFFICIENCY: Low maintenance – just pruning (see below) – and can be very productive if the blossom escapes the frosts and the fruit stays out of beaks.

GROWING: To avoid silver leaf, prune during the growing season but wait until after harvesting. With sweet cherries, the aim is to maintain an open-centred goblet shape with a balance of wood that is at least one year old and some new replacement branches

– it is largely about removing crossing, weak or diseased wood. Acid cherries such as 'Morello' fruit largely on the previous year's wood, so while a goblet shape is still the aim, acid cherries need to be pruned to maintain a balance of last year's wood and new growth to replace it. Cutting back around a quarter of newly fruited wood to a new shoot in late summer causes the tree to throw more energy into these new replacement shoots. Cut any central growth back to a good side shoot to keep the centre open.

Cherries can be trained into many shapes, but a fan offers the dual benefits of utilising a sheltered spot and ease of netting from birds. Water in dry spells as cherries are quite shallow rooting. Give an annual mulch of compost or manure.

POTENTIAL PROBLEMS: Cherries are early flowering so give them (particularly the sweet cherries) a sheltered spot. Birds will love your cherries as much as you, especially if a sweet variety. 'Duke', 'Morello' and white varieties of cherry are less troubled by the birds. Bacterial canker and silver leaf are the most common diseases encountered.

HARVEST: At the height of summer, pick and eat whilst warm from the tree.

CHILEAN GUAVA

Myrtus ugni or *Ugni molinae*. Half-hardy evergreen shrub.

Not the hefty, tropical guava familiar from the shops, but a deliciously sweet/sharp berry that's even more welcome ripening as it does in the depths of late autumn. It was Queen Victoria's favourite fruit, which is saying something given she appears grumpy enough not to have many favourites of anything. Their flavour is like a raspberry and blackcurrant and blueberry combined – I tend to eat most of them straight from the bush, but they're great in muffins and fools too.

VARIETIES: Most sold as a generic Chilean guava, but you might find the variegated 'Flambeau' or yellow-leaved 'Butterball'. Self-fertile.

STARTING OFF: Source plants from good suppliers. Propagate by taking cuttings or layering, or from seed in autumn or spring.

POSITION: Naturally a woodland edge plant so tolerant of some shade. It needs shelter from cold winds and good drainage. It is hardy down to –10°C when dormant so may need taking under cover in more northerly regions. Tolerant of most soils.

SPACING: 2.5m apart.

PRODUCTIVITY/EFFICIENCY: Chilean guava will provide you with fruit in early winter and with little input.

GROWING: Just prune for shape if and when you fancy, and a handful of manure or a liquid feed now and again to boost your crop.

POTENTIAL PROBLEMS: Generally pest and disease free.

HARVEST: Pick fruits as they ripen in late autumn/early winter.

CHOCOLATE VINE

Akebia quinata. Hardy evergreen climber.

A wonderful plant for growing over or along a structure to add interest throughout the year – it has glossy leaves borne in fives that cling to the plant all year. Flowers come in spring and early summer, and have a gorgeous chocolatey scent. In a good year – or under cover – these will be followed by fat pods. Pop these pods open to reveal a centre filled with a translucent pulp (that tastes mildly of cool melon) and big seeds – suck in the former and spit out the latter.

VARIETIES: Usually sold as its generic form. Even though Akebia plants have both male and female flowers, having two plants greatly increases the likelihood of pollination occurring.

STARTING OFF: Source plants from a specialist supplier or sow seed in modules in spring.

POSITION: Tolerant of most moist but well-drained soils. Likes full sun or partial shade.

SPACING: Can climb to 10m high and will reach 40cm wide.

PRODUCTIVITY/EFFICIENCY: A beautiful plant but a little reluctant to fruit in a cooler climate.

GROWING: Provide support – perhaps through the crown of a tree as in the wild. Prune whenever you like to keep growth at a lower level if you prefer. Makes a great hedge twining through a fence or other plants.

POTENTIAL PROBLEMS: Generally pest and disease free.

HARVEST: Young, soft shoots can be eaten throughout the growing season (steam them briefly and serve as a dressed side dish) and fruits are harvested in autumn. The soft pulp inside the fruit won't keep, so eat it straight away.

C

CRANBERRIES

Vaccinium macrocarpon. Evergreen shrub.

When grown commercially in the USA, cranberries are harvested by flooding. A huge bund is built around the plantation and flooded with water at harvest time – the dislodged cranberries float to the surface and are sieved off to market. It's not likely you'll grow them on that scale, or have the acidic soil conditions they need, so it's best to grow them in containers where the pH is easy to control. The berries themselves are wonderfully sharp, sour and juicy, classically cooked into a sauce in a little orange juice, and sweetened with honey or sugar, and port added once softened. They're really good too added to tarts and other puddings to punctuate with their sharpness – and once you start using them, you'll find plenty more excuses to use them.

VARIETIES: Try 'Early Black' or 'Pilgrim' for berries in August. You could also try *Vaccinium vitis-idaea*, commonly known as the lingonberry, which has similar requirements (see page 152). Self-fertile.

STARTING OFF: Source plants from specialist suppliers or layer established plants in spring and early autumn.

POSITION: Cranberries need an acidic soil, with a pH of 4–4.5. They will grow well in moist and boggy soils, and soils with a high peat content. They are most fruitful in poor soils. They can also be grown in containers and hanging baskets using ericaceous compost.

SPACING: 30cm apart.

PRODUCTIVITY/EFFICIENCY: A very good groundcover plant needing little attention. Plants will begin to fruit in their fourth or fifth year and can go on fruiting for up to 100 years.

GROWING: Water with rainwater. Little pruning needed other than removing damaged shoots. They dislike root disturbance.

POTENTIAL PROBLEMS: Cover to protect crops from birds.

HARVEST: Pick when fruits have a reached a deep colour.

ELDER

Sambucus species. Deciduous shrub or tree.

There are few plants that highlight the turning of the seasons as well as the elder. I can't imagine there could be spring into summer without their flowers, nor a summer into autumn without their berries. Whether you're in the city or countryside, chances are elder is not far from you – it will grow on any rough ground and can be found in field boundaries here and there. It's easy to grow in your garden too, with common, unusual and particularly ornamental varieties available.

VARIETIES: *S. nigra* is the UK's native species and 'Haschberg', 'Ina' and 'Sampo' are heavily flowering and fruiting varieties. You could also try *S. racemosa*, which makes a smaller tree and tolerates considerable shade, or *S. canadensis*, which produces a succession of flower heads from July to November.

STARTING OFF: Source named varieties from a good supplier or propagate from hardwood cuttings.

POSITION: Tolerant of most soils, although a moist rich soil is its natural preference.

SPACING: Can reach 6m wide but are easily pruned (see below) to fit a smaller space.

PRODUCTIVITY/EFFICIENCY: Valuable for its heavy crops of flowers and berries from its second year. Elder makes a very good hedge.

GROWING: Prune as and when you fancy to control size if desired.

POTENTIAL PROBLEMS: Generally pest and disease free.

HARVEST: Flowers are ready in late May/early June and are most fragrant when the sun is shining on them. Berries are ready in August and September, and are easily harvested with a harvesting comb (or failing that, a fork) into a container.

FIGS

Ficus carica. Deciduous shrub or tree.

The finest fig I've ever eaten was a few summers ago, not, as you might imagine, in the heat of the Mediterranean, but in the comparative cool of Tottenham, North London. Chris Achilleos has possibly the most incredible allotment I've ever seen; a sheltered garden of edible and ornamental delights, with cricket ball-sized figs that were splitting under the burden of their own ripeness. Succulent, sweet and with the most sublime depth of flavour, these figs made me plant a couple more, in as sheltered and sunny a spot as I could find, when I got home.

VARIETIES: 'Brown Turkey', 'Brunswick' and 'White Marseilles' are reliable croppers outside in an English climate. Try 'Rouge de Bordeaux' or 'Precoce de Dalmatie' if growing in a sunny, sheltered spot. Self-fertile.

STARTING OFF: Source plants from a good supplier or propagate from hardwood cuttings.

POSITION: Good drainage and sun. Roots will need restricting to promote fruiting, so they're very much one to grow in containers.

SPACING: 4–5m apart.

PRODUCTIVITY/EFFICIENCY: This is a very low maintenance plant that can give 15kg of fruit in good conditions.

GROWING: Can be grown as a bush or trained against a wall as a fan. Give plants an annual mulch of compost or manure.

POTENTIAL PROBLEMS: Generally pest and disease free. Keep container-grown figs moist throughout growing season to prevent fruits from dropping.

HARVEST: Pick fruit when they soften and droop. They won't ripen further when picked.

FUCHSIA

Fuchsia species. Evergreen shrub behaving as a herbaceous perennial in colder areas.

You won't get fruit from a fuchsia every year unless you are in the most sheltered and sunny spot, but when they come you'll be very glad of them. In a sunny summer, those awful, gaudy flowers will turn into long fruity batons, with a flavour somewhere between kiwi, strawberry and blackcurrant, with just a hint of pepper. After a few years, you can pick plenty – I'm hoping to try fuchsia ice cream next year – but early on you're unlikely to get a harvest large enough to do much with, but when they are hard to beat just eaten fresh from the bush, who cares?

VARIETIES: All species are edible but *Fuchsia magellanica* is the hardiest. 'Riccartonii' is particularly hardy with scarlet-purple berries, and 'Globosa' is very productive. Self-fertile.

STARTING OFF: Source plants from a good supplier or buy semi-ripe cuttings in late summer.

POSITION: A well-drained soil in sun or partial shade, avoiding frost pockets. They do well in coastal areas.

SPACING: 3m apart.

PRODUCTIVITY/EFFICIENCY: Very little work needed for a good crop of berries.

GROWING: In colder areas mulch around base of plants in winter. Cut out deadwood in spring.

POTENTIAL PROBLEMS: Net against birds if a nuisance.

HARVEST: Pick fruits when dark and softening.

GOJI BERRIES

Lycium barbarum. Also known as: wolfberries. Deciduous shrub.

Fresh goji berries are a pleasure I've yet to really appreciate, but dried, which is how most are available in the shops, they are rather fine. Be aware: gojis will grow for any fool but what they give in ease, they take in space, sprawling upwards and across with vigour. They are perfectly lovely, and perfect in a large garden, but perhaps not the first choice for container growing or for those with limited space as they want to go bonkers.

VARIETIES: There are few named cultivars; 'Crimson Star' is one that you might find. Self-fertile.

STARTING OFF: Source plants from a good supplier. You can also grow from seed or dig up new plants that are made when shoot tips touch the ground.

POSITION: Fruits best in full sun and is tolerant of most soils.

SPACING: 3m apart.

PRODUCTIVITY/EFFICIENCY: Goji berries start fruiting in year 2 or 3 and need little work.

GROWING: Cut back hard in winter if you want to control its sprawling growth, and be aware that the branches will root where they touch soil – ideal for creating new plants, but to be avoided if you don't want them to spread.

POTENTIAL PROBLEMS: Generally pest and disease free.

HARVEST: Goji berries ripen steadily from summer into autumn. Pick when fully coloured.

GOOSEBERRIES

Ribes uva-crispa. Deciduous shrub.

Gooseberries are the best of both worlds as far as fruit are concerned – early and sharp, or late and sweet – and I love both equally. The first crop usually goes to make sharp sauces (perfect with mackerel), and pureed for knickerbocker glories and to go with the early summer elderflower; the sweeter, late picking for crumbles and ice creams. Picking half of the berries early allows the rest of the plant's energies to ripen the remaining gooseberries more easily.

VARIETIES: 'Invicta' is very productive and delicious – good for both cooking and eating fresh. You could try 'Hinnomaki Red' or 'Redeva' for lovely sweet red berries.

STARTING OFF: Source plants from a good supplier or take hardwood cuttings in winter.

POSITION: Gooseberries can fruit in a shady spot but will produce more in the sun.

SPACING: 1.5m apart.

PRODUCTIVITY/EFFICIENCY: A gooseberry can give up to 4kg of fruit in good conditions, and asks very little of you.

GROWING: An annual mulch of compost or manure will get the most out of your gooseberry. Most commonly grown as bushes, gooseberries can also be grown as cordons, standards or fan trained. For bushes and standards, prune new growth back to 5 leaves in summer to encourage fruit buds; in winter prune side shoots back to around 2 buds from the base and shorten branches by a quarter, cutting to an outward-facing bud to maintain a good framework. For cordons and fans, prune side shoots back to 5 leaves in summer and then again to 1 or 2 buds in winter.

POTENTIAL PROBLEMS: Choose resistant varieties (some, such as 'Invicta', have at least partial resistance) to avoid powdery mildew.

HARVEST: Gooseberries can be harvested in May when they're sharp, primarily for cooking, and in June and July when some can be sweet enough for eating fresh.

GRAPES

Vitis vinifera. Deciduous climber.

A grape vine is a mightily impressive plant. Buy one small and within a few years it'll have formed a woody framework along or over whatever you train it against, and - in most years at least - it will give you many bunches of delicious fruit. Choose your varieties well - for eating, wine, or both - as they can be productive for decades.

VARIETIES: 'Phoenix' is an excellent white variety for eating and winemaking, 'Boskoop Glory' is a reliable producer outside, with good black grapes for eating. 'Madeleine Angevine' is a late-flowering variety for winemakers in colder areas. If you have a greenhouse in a sunny spot, you could try 'Muscat Alexandria'. Self-fertile.

STARTING OFF: Source grafted plants from a good supplier.

POSITION: A very sunny spot with shelter if possible. Vines prefer a moist but well-drained soil. They can be grown in containers, but don't neglect feeding and watering.

SPACING: Vines are vigorous and can climb up to 30m, but they can also be pruned to fit into a small space.

PRODUCTIVITY/EFFICIENCY: The size of your crop will depend to a large extent on the space you allocate to your vine.

GROWING: Prune to keep a manageable size. Take off leaves that shade grape bunches.

POTENTIAL PROBLEMS: Ensure good ventilation in your site choice to avoid powdery and downy mildew.

HARVEST: Fruits ripen from August to October, depending on variety. Don't forget to pick tender young leaves for eating (especially good as dolmades, stuffed with rice) before late spring/early summer. The best are those that are about three leaves down from the tip on the young shoots.

HAWTHORN

Crataegus species. Deciduous tree.

One of the most common of our hedgerow plants, and well worth adding to your own if there are none nearby to plunder. I love the flowers' perfume (though one of the two common wild kinds has a perfume more like cat's pee than the other) even more than the berries, but the berries are a fine autumnal treat, especially made into haw ketchup.

VARIETIES: Many hawthorns are edible and *C. ellwangeriana* and *C. schraderiana*, amongst others, have fruit that is good raw as well as cooked. All species are self-fertile.

STARTING OFF: Source grafted plants from a good supplier.

POSITION: Grafted plants will be happy in most soils and like some sun to fruit well.

SPACING: Mature trees can reach 5m high by 4m wide.

PRODUCTIVITY/EFFICIENCY: Plants usually start fruiting around year three.

GROWING: Little maintenance required, though will happily take to trimming or pruning in winter for shape.

POTENTIAL PROBLEMS: Generally pest and disease free.

HARVEST: Pick fruits as they begin to soften in September or October.

HAZEL

Corylus species. Deciduous shrub or tree.

Hazels are fairly widespread in our hedgerows, but the very finest varieties are so much better in flavour and texture that I'd urge you to find space for one if you can. As well as fine nuts in autumn (white filberts are my very favourites), hazels provide sticks for garden supports, with their catkins lighting up their corner in the cold months.

VARIETIES: Hazelnuts are either *Corylus avellana* (hazel), *C. maxima* (filbert) or a cross between the two. Try 'Gunselbert' or 'Butler' for good flavoured and productive trees. Hazels are partially self-fertile and will produce bigger crops with cross-pollination.

STARTING OFF: Source trees from a specialist – they are usually supplied on their own rootstock.

POSITION: Hazels fruit best in full sun and need a well-drained soil. They are wind pollinated.

SPACING: Around 6m apart or half that for hedges.

PRODUCTIVITY/EFFICIENCY: Hazels are good value, with a mature tree producing around 5kg of nuts each year. It is worth coppicing hazels if you have more than one as the poles make good plant supports. Just bear in mind it will take the coppiced tree a couple of years or so to start producing nuts again.

GROWING: Hazels grown as single-stemmed trees may produce suckers and it's best to cut these out during the summer.

POTENTIAL PROBLEMS: Squirrels will need controlling if in your area.

HARVEST: Hazelnuts are ready in September. Collect them from the ground or pick from the tree. Hazelnuts usually keep for a few months in their shell; dried in a dehydrator they will keep for several years; after roasting for 15–20 minutes at 140°C or so they will keep their flavour and texture frozen for at least a year.

JAPANESE PLUMS

Prunus salicina. Deciduous tree.

A really beautiful and flavoursome change from the plums we know and love, Japanese plums blossom early and ripen in July, well ahead of most tree fruit. So full of blossom and fruitfulness are they, that they haven't the spare energy to get beyond five feet or so tall, which makes them great for a small garden. The fruit is juicy, sweet and meaty – substantial and bold, and highly recommended.

VARIETIES: Try self-fertile 'Methley' for reddish-purple fruits ripening in July, or 'Shiro' for large, sweet yellow fruit in July (also self-fertile). Some Japanese plums are partially self-fertile and will produce more with another pollinator nearby. European plums don't pollinate Japanese plums.

STARTING OFF: Source grafted plants from a good supplier.

POSITION: Grow in a warm, sheltered place as this species of plum flowers early.

SPACING: 4m apart.

PRODUCTIVITY/EFFICIENCY: At full production, a Japanese plum tree can give you up to 40kg of fruit.

GROWING: Create a good, nicely spread branch structure in early years, pruning in summer after fruiting, cutting out dead and diseased wood in subsequent summers. You should also thin out fruit in the early years so that the tree isn't overly burdened. Give trees an annual mulch of compost or manure in late winter/early spring.

POTENTIAL PROBLEMS: Less affected by pests and disease than its European counterpart.

HARVEST: Pick the fruits when the aroma and flavour are well developed.

JAPANESE QUINCE

Chaenomeles species. Also known as: oriental quince. Deciduous shrub.

I used to think of these as quince for anyone who hasn't the space for a familiar quince tree, but the more I use them the more I think of them as their own glorious thing. The fruit, hard and unforgiving as quinces are at first, are like a slightly smaller version of their namesake, but with a spiciness and zing of their own. Whereas quinces are very much autumnal, Chaenomeles have one foot still in summer. Try them juiced, with plenty of balancing sugar and water, for a refreshing summer drink.

VARIETIES: There are many varieties bred mainly for their ornamental characteristics. 'Jet Trail' and 'Crimson and Gold' are both beautiful and productive. Self-fertile.

STARTING OFF: Source plants from a specialist nursery.

POSITION: Tolerant of most soils and a fair amount of shade. The flowers are quite frost tolerant too.

SPACING: 2–5m, depending on variety.

PRODUCTIVITY/EFFICIENCY: Chaenomeles will provide you with many unbuyable fruits for little maintenance.

GROWING: A little pruning for shape, if and when you fancy, is all they require.

POTENTIAL PROBLEMS: Generally disease and pest free.

HARVEST: Fruit is ready in September to October and will keep for several weeks.

JAPANESE WINEBERRIES

Rubus phoenicolasius. Deciduous shrub.

Wineberries are one of my very few desert island plants. Productive and delicious, low-maintenance and unbuyable, they also add colour and structure to the garden in the depths of winter when there's little else to catch the eye. The pink/purple-furred canes grow one year, sprouting fruiting side shoots the next, catching the winter sun when most other plants have disappeared into the cold. The fruit itself is fabulous – a fuller, winier version of a raspberry – and at its most prolific between the peaks of summer and autumn raspberries.

VARIETIES: No named varieties. Self-fertile.

STARTING OFF: Source plants from a good supplier or propagate by seed, hardwood cuttings or layering stem tips.

POSITION: Wineberries are happy in shade but fruit best in a sunny spot. They are tolerant of most soils.

SPACING: 2m apart.

PRODUCTIVITY/EFFICIENCY: With very little work effort on your part, wineberries will provide you with a steady supply of fruit from July to September.

GROWING: Cut old fruited stems to the ground. The odd mulch of compost or manure will be appreciated.

POTENTIAL PROBLEMS: Generally pest and disease free.

HARVEST: Pick when the protective hairy calyxes have opened out.

JOSTABERRIES

Ribes x culverwellii. Deciduous shrub.

A cross between a gooseberry and blackcurrant, with the best of both in its flavour, jostaberries make a great choice if you have room for only one of the others, or indeed if you've got space for all three. Get out those blackcurrant and gooseberry recipes and try them with jostaberries instead – spot on.

VARIETIES: No named varieties. Self-fertile.

STARTING OFF: Source bare-root or pot-grown plants from a good supplier. Jostaberries can also be propagated by hardwood cuttings.

POSITION: Tolerant of most soils and some shade. Jostaberries can be grown successfully in containers.

SPACING: 2m apart.

PRODUCTIVITY/EFFICIENCY: Jostaberries are fast growers, reaching full size (2–3m) and production in 4 years or so. They will provide you with heavy yields of large fruit for around 15 years.

GROWING: Give an annual mulch of compost or manure. Prune in winter as you would blackcurrants to give a supply of new fruit-bearing wood.

POTENTIAL PROBLEMS: Good pest and disease resistance.

HARVEST: Harvest around June/July. As with the gooseberry you can harvest at various stages depending on whether you are cooking or eating fresh.

JUNEBERRY

Amelanchier species. Deciduous tree.

A beautiful shrub or tree with striking thin-petalled flowers in spring, followed by dark purple/black currant-sized berries in early summer. Allow them to ripen and soften before eating - their flavour is quite similar to blackcurrants but sweeter. They're really good as they are, and take to preserving well - making fruit leathers especially.

VARIETIES: Many of the Amelanchier species produce edible fruit. *A. canadensis* is the serviceberry but you could also try *A. lamarckii* 'Ballerina', or *A. alnifolia*, the large-fruited saskatoon.

STARTING OFF: Source plants from a specialist supplier.

POSITION: Sun or part-shade and happy in most soils.

SPACING: Plants can reach 6m high and 4m wide.

PRODUCTIVITY/EFFICIENCY: Trees start producing fruit in their second or third year, and fruit is ready to harvest in July. Easy and beautiful.

GROWING: Little or no maintenance required.

POTENTIAL PROBLEMS: Generally pest and disease free, but watch out for the birds when the fruit ripens – may require netting.

HARVEST: Fruit are ready to pick in July when dark purple and slightly soft.

KIWIS

Actinidia species. Deciduous climber.

The full-size kiwis most of us are familiar with need room - a single plant can reach 5m or so in each direction with little encouragement, and you need male and female plants to produce fruit. They are beautiful and, if trained properly (as you would a grape), very fruitful. A better bet for most are the dwarf varieties, aka hardy or self-fertile varieties. These dwarfs will reach only 2-3m in spread and produce plenty of grape-sized kiwis, ripening late in autumn and into winter. They are as delicious as the full-sized varieties and (weird as it may seem) you can eat them furry skin and all - it dissolves in a second.

VARIETIES: There are three species of edible kiwi: *Actinidia arguta*, *A. deliciosa* and *A. kolomikta*. Generally speaking, plants are either male or female and you will need a male plant for pollination of the female to take place. More recently, however, there are some self-fertile varieties available. *A. arguta* is very hardy and good varieties to try are the dwarf 'Issai' (self-fertile) or 'Jumbo' (long large fruits), the latter of which will need a male plant like 'Weiki' for pollination. If you have a sheltered warm spot, try self-fertile dwarf *A. deliciosa* 'Jenny' or the full-size 'Hayward' with a male pollinator 'Tomuri'.

STARTING OFF: Source a self-fertile or female with male pollinator from a specialist supplier. Suppliers will tell you if and which pollinator is required.

POSITION: Tolerant of most soils, but do plant in a sheltered spot and avoid frost pockets.

SPACING: Kiwis can be trained horizontally to fit the space available to you.

PRODUCTIVITY/EFFICIENCY: Very many fruits are produced by a single plant, from September to November. Large kiwis should be up to full production in 4–5 years; dwarf/self-fertile varieties much more quickly.

GROWING: Pruning is needed to control vigour. Fruit is borne on new growth arising from older canes. Canes become less productive after 3 years so prune out one or two 4-year-old canes each year whilst the plant is dormant to stimulate fresh growth. Apply a good mulch of compost or manure each spring.

POTENTIAL PROBLEMS: Protect young plants from slugs, snails and cats, but other than that they are generally pest and disease free.

HARVEST: Pick fruits when very slightly under-ripe; left too long they become slightly alcoholic in taste and slushy in texture.

LINGONBERRIES

Vaccinium vitis-idaea. Also known as: mountain berry or cowberry. Evergreen shrub.

A popular foraged berry in Scandinavia and grown commercially in the States, the lingonberry is pretty uncommon in the UK. That will change: they are simply too good. They sit somewhere near cranberries on the taste spectrum, making excellent jams, sauces and to add zip to flapjacks and other biscuits and cakes, and they go really well in savoury dishes, with chicken especially.

VARIETIES: Try 'Ida' or 'Red Pearl'. Self-fertile.

STARTING OFF: Source from a good supplier and propagate by division or layering.

POSITION: Moist, acidic soils and ideal for a cooler climate. Lingonberries grow well in containers with ericaceous compost.

SPACING: 50cm apart (30cm for ground cover and dwarf varieties).

PRODUCTIVITY/EFFICIENCY: These make good groundcover plants to suppress weeds. Lingonberries usually fruit in their first year and are fully productive by their third year.

GROWING: Lingonberries are drought tolerant and need very little maintenance. Use rainwater if watering is necessary, as tap water is more alkaline.

POTENTIAL PROBLEMS: None.

HARVEST: Lingonberries flower twice. If a late frost doesn't get the first flush of flowers you will have fruit in late July and then again in late September.

MEDLAR

Mespilus germanica. Deciduous tree.

If you're after something that fruits reliably every year, requires no maintenance, and where the fruit is both unbuyable and delicious, the medlar should be on your list. Looking like an apple with a more open end, medlars have a flavour somewhere between cooking apples and dates – sharp and deep at the same time. They are best used when bletted: when the pale apple flesh begins to break down, soften and darken. Bletting draws out the deep winey side of their flavour and smooths out any sharpness. They are fabulous for jellies, jams and all manner of puddings.

VARIETIES: I've never been able to tell any varieties apart for flavour, although 'Large Russian' has larger fruit than most. 'Westerveld' and 'Nottingham' are both commonly available and excellent. Medlar 'Seedless' has slightly smaller fruits and considerably fewer seeds. Self-fertile.

STARTING OFF: Source grafted plants from a good supplier.

POSITION: Tolerant of shade, but will fruit better in full sun. Moisture-retentive but well-drained soil.

SPACING: Around 5m, depending on rootstock.

PRODUCTIVITY/EFFICIENCY: Mature medlar trees can produce up to 20kg of fruit and begin fruiting in their second or third year.

GROWING: Little maintenance required. Pruning isn't necessary.

POTENTIAL PROBLEMS: Generally pest and disease free.

HARVEST: Pick when softening after the first frosts. They can be picked earlier and ripened inside.

MELONS

Cucumis melo. Half-hardy annual.

Melons are something of a gamble – they'll need a good summer and a sunny, sheltered spot, ideally under cover, to fruit. That said, what's to lose – a few seeds and a little time and compost – when the reward can be beautifully ripe, sun-warmed fruit, bursting with juice. If the year is good and my luck's in, I eat almost all of them fresh as they are, though the odd one might make it into a sorbet or cocktail.

VARIETIES: 'Minnesota Midget' and 'Queen Anne's Pocket' are flavoursome small melons, or try cantaloupe 'HoneyBun'. If you have a heated greenhouse you could try muskmelon 'Blenheim Orange' or the watermelon 'Sugar Baby'. Self-fertile.

STARTING OFF: Sow in 9cm pots under cover, about 6 weeks before the last frosts, and plant in a mound of soil to prevent the stem becoming too wet. If planting outside, warm the soil for a few weeks first using a cloche or black plastic, and harden the plant off.

POSITION: Somewhere warm and sunny, preferably under cover with a moisture-retentive, humus-rich soil with good drainage.

SPACING: 50cm apart if growing vertically, and between 1–1.5m apart if plants are scrambling.

PRODUCTIVITY/EFFICIENCY: You will get around 4 or 5 melons per plant (more for smaller varieties).

GROWING: Plants can be grown on the flat, pinching out after 5 leaves have developed and allowing 4 lateral shoots to grow. For trained melons, allow a single stem to grow and pinch out when 2m tall, and then pinch out each lateral after 5 leaves. Side shoots growing from laterals will carry the fruit. Melons suspended in the air will need supporting with netting, tights or similar. Allow only 4 or 5 melons to develop (more for varieties producing smaller melons).

Water and feed regularly with comfrey tea or similar. You may need to help pollination along by using a soft dry brush between flowers – each plant has both male and female flowers.

POTENTIAL PROBLEMS: Use a biological treatment if red spider mite is a problem. Keep soil moist to avoid powdery mildew.

HARVEST: Pick when fruits smell aromatic and leave to ripen indoors for a few more days for the best flavour.

MIRABELLE PLUMS

Prunus cerasifera. Also known as: cherry plums. Deciduous tree.

Mirabelles are strangely under-appreciated in the UK while being popular on the continent. Certainly they need a good spring with the early blossom avoiding frosts, but once past that potential trouble time, there's nothing between you and delicious, early mirabelles. If you've not eaten them before, expect small but juicy and flavoursome plums ready to pick before most other plums.

VARIETIES: Try 'Golden Sphere' for yellow fruit and 'Gypsy' for red, both being partially self-fertile. 'Mirabelle de Nancy' is self-fertile and produces small sweet fruit.

STARTING OFF: Source grafted plants from a specialist supplier.

POSITION: Tolerant of most situations, but fruits best in sun and with some shelter from winds.

SPACING: Between 2.5–7m, depending on rootstock.

PRODUCTIVITY/EFFICIENCY: Mirabelle plums can crop heavily and need little maintenance to remain productive.

GROWING: Give plants an annual mulch of compost or manure. Prune out only dead and crossing branches.

POTENTIAL PROBLEMS: Prune from late spring into summer to avoid silver leaf.

HARVEST: Pick fruits as they soften, and their flavour and aroma develops – often as early as July, or as late as September, depending on variety.

MULBERRIES

Morus species. Deciduous tree.

My favourite fruit. Every year when I eat them, I'm surprised they surpass the peaches that come in midsummer, or the first strawberries, but every year they do. Picked at their dark peak, their flavour is deep and complex – raspberry, blackcurrant and blackberry, with a little sherbet. So laden are they with deep purple juice, that you can expect your hands and clothes to be covered: dress appropriately. It is this abundance of juiciness that keeps them from the shops; it's impossible to pick them at this peak and get them to the shops (much less to your home) with them in one piece. Avoid the compact, dwarf mulberries: what they offer in productivity, they lack in flavour.

VARIETIES: Morus species include *M. alba*, *M. nigra* and *M. rubra*. Mulberries can take many years to fruit, but some of the quickest are from *M. alba* x *M. rubra* crosses. Try 'Illinois Everbearing', which fruits in 2–3 years and crops over a long period, or 'Carman', which produces white fruit from a young age. *M. nigra* 'King James' (aka 'Chelsea') produces very big, black mulberries. *M. alba* 'Agate' produces huge, flavoursome, black fruits. All species are self-fertile.

STARTING OFF: Source plants from a good supplier or propagate from semi-ripe cuttings.

POSITION: Needs some sun and shelter, but is tolerant of most soils. Mulberries can be grown in large containers.

SPACING: Up to 10m, depending on cultivar and if allowed to grow to full size. Size can be restricted by pruning in summer.

PRODUCTIVITY/EFFICIENCY: Mulberries will crop heavily over a long period of time once established. Trees are slow-growing, so reasonable crops can take several years.

GROWING: Mulch thickly around the base for the first couple of years and water well until established. Prune out any dead or diseased wood in winter.

POTENTIAL PROBLEMS: Protect young plants from slugs and snails.

HARVEST: Fruits are soft and don't keep. Hand-pick when deeply coloured, or spread a sheet around the base of the tree and gently shake the branches. Fruit will ripen over a long period so harvest often. *Morus alba* species have the best leaves for eating, stuffed with whatever filling you fancy.

NEPALESE RASPBERRIES

Rubus nepalensis. Also known as: Himalayan creeping bramble. Frost-tender evergreen.

A fantastic evergreen creeping fruit that colonises ground relatively quickly. The glossy, deep-green leaves and deep-red berries make for a beautiful plant that's pretty rufty-tufty too – it won't complain if you walk on it now and again. The berries come in summer and, though rarely prolific, are very good: quite raspberry-like.

VARIETIES: Available only in its generic form. Self-fertile.

STARTING OFF: Source plants from a specialist supplier. Plants can also be grown from seed by sowing in modules in autumn and left in a cold frame, or by dividing established plants in spring.

POSITION: Grows best in a frost-free, semi-shady spot. Prefers moist but well-drained soil.

SPACING: Plant 1m apart for relatively fast ground cover.

PRODUCTIVITY/EFFICIENCY: A low-maintenance plant that makes a good weed-suppressing ground cover, and that will also provide you with fruit in late summer.

GROWING: No maintenance required.

POTENTIAL PROBLEMS: Generally pest and disease free.

HARVEST: Berries are ready for harvesting from July to August.

OLIVES

Olea europaea. Borderline hardy tree.

Not one to grow if you're after a cast-iron guarantee of a harvest, but perhaps beautiful enough to take the gamble on. Shelter and sunshine are essentials to a healthy plant, never mind fruit; with those and a well-drained soil you may get lucky and harvest more than a few fruit in autumn. Choice of variety is very important (see below) as is ensuring that your plant hasn't spent most of its life somewhere far sunnier than where you plan for it - like you would, it'll complain long and hard if uprooted from the balmy heat of Tuscany for the chilly wilds of North Yorkshire.

VARIETIES: 'Arbequina' makes a small tree, and begins fruiting early in its life as well as ripening earlier than many other varieties. You could also try 'Frantoio', 'Leccino' and 'Maurino', which all hail from northern Italy. Olives need another variety available for pollination and are wind pollinated so need planting fairly near to each other.

STARTING OFF: Source plants from a good supplier, ensuring they are of a variety and strain suitable for your climate.

POSITION: Tolerant of a wide range of soils but free drainage is a must. Give olives the sunniest spot you have, and shelter from easterly and northerly winds. Olives are very suitable for containers.

SPACING: Olives can be pruned to fit the space available.

PRODUCTIVITY/EFFICIENCY: Varieties such as 'Arbequina' can start producing olives early in their lives, whilst others may take up to 12 years. The size of harvest is likely to be variable in the UK, dependant on the weather and the shelter afforded to your trees.

GROWING: Undertake light, formative pruning in spring and aim for an open goblet shape. Remove all suckers from the base of the tree. If growing in a pot, feed fortnightly with a liquid seaweed or comfrey feed, and when potting on only go up slightly in size.

POTENTIAL PROBLEMS: Pruning early in the year ensures wounds heal sufficiently before winter. If your winter temperatures routinely drop below −5°C then wrap the trunk and crown of your olives in horticultural fleece in their early years. Pots will need insulating with bubble wrap too or bringing inside.

HARVEST: Harvesting will be somewhere between October and January, and when the olives are slightly soft when squeezed. They will need to be soaked and then brined before they can be eaten.

PEACHES AND NECTARINES

Prunus persica. Deciduous tree.

Both peaches and nectarines need sun and shelter, yet even with both are far from assured harvests each year, but the fruit are so special you'll be glad you took the risk when they do produce. Most peaches in the shops are picked early and firm to allow them time to be transported to the shelves and ripen at home - their texture and flavour never quite recovers from that early harvesting. Grow them yourself and you'll find it very hard to enjoy those from the shops again.

VARIETIES: 'Red Haven' and 'Rochester' peaches are delicious and reasonably resistant to leaf curl; 'Pineapple' nectarine is sweet and delicious. You could also try the dwarf nectarine 'Nectarella' or dwarf peach 'Bonanza'. Peaches and nectarines are self-fertile.

STARTING OFF: Source grafted plants from a good supplier.

POSITION: Full sun in a sheltered position, and moisture-retentive and well-drained soil. Peaches grow well in containers and will fruit well planted inside a polytunnel or greenhouse. Nectarines will fare best against a wall.

SPACING: Between 3–5m apart, and less for dwarf plants.

PRODUCTIVITY/EFFICIENCY: Yields may vary considerably depending on the summer, though in a good year can produce up to 35kg of fruit (14kg for a fan). Trees will begin to produce in their second or third year.

GROWING: Diseased and dead wood should be pruned out in summer after fruiting. Prune fan-trained peaches and nectarines in summer – fruit forms largely on shoots formed the previous year, so fruited wood should be replaced each year with new growth. Provide with an annual mulch of compost or manure.

POTENTIAL PROBLEMS: Leaf curl is the biggest problem in a damp climate. Grow resistant varieties such as 'Rochester' (despite claims to the contrary none are that resistant) and if possible protect plants from spring rains in particular. You may need to help pollination along by using a soft brush, especially if growing under cover.

HARVEST: The fruits are ready in mid- to late summer, when aromatic, soft and leave the tree with the merest gentle persuasion.

PEARS

Pyrus communis. Deciduous tree.

I'm busy planting a few more pears here this winter; we've half a dozen or so, but we eat so many it's time to have some more that produce at either end of the season - early and late - so that we can enjoy them for more of the year. For me, pears are a perfect candidate for growing as trained fruit - espaliers, stepovers and cordons in particular. Few are self-fertile, so planting cordons that take little room gives you the possibility of pears in even a small space.

VARIETIES: As with apples, there are dessert and culinary as well as perry pears (for making perry). Try the old English culinary 'Black Worcester' or old French 'Catillac'. Try the late season 'Conference' and 'Doyenne du Comice' dessert pears, which are both reliable in the UK. Or try 'Beurre Giffard' for an aromatic pear ready to eat in August.

Pears need a pollinator to bear fruit; even those that are self-fertile will bear heavier crops with a pollinator. If space is limited you could try a 'family' tree with several varieties grafted on to a single stem. Choose varieties in compatible pollination groups, but watch out for the ones that won't pollinate other specific varieties, e.g. 'Doyenne du Comice' and 'Onward' are poor partners even though they are in adjacent groups.

STARTING OFF: Source grafted plants from a good supplier.

POSITION: A sunny, sheltered position. The main rootstocks used are tolerant of a wide range of soils, with the exception of Quince C, which prefers a fertile soil.

SPACING: 2.5–8m apart, depending on rootstock.

PRODUCTIVITY/EFFICIENCY: Pears can take between 3–10 years to begin bearing fruit, and can yield between 15–100kg once fully producing, depending on rootstock.

GROWING: Pears take well to training and can be trained as fans, cordons and stepovers. Undertake formative pruning in winter. Prune trained trees in summer: any new shoots over 20cm should be cut back to three leaves above the cluster that forms at the base. Give plants an annual mulch of compost or manure, except those on a pear rootstock, which don't need it.

POTENTIAL PROBLEMS: Choose varieties resistant to canker, fireblight and scab. Cut out any limbs affected by fireblight and burn, disinfecting your saw afterwards.

HARVEST: It is important not to leave the pears for too long on the tree or they risk becoming 'sleepy' (grainy, soft and perhaps brown) in storage. Test the pears for readiness as their time for ripeness approaches by holding the bulbous end of the pear in your palm and, with your index finger on the stalk, gently tilt the fruit upwards; it will come away easily if ready. Only the earliest pears will be ready to eat from the tree. Later-ripening varieties will be ready several weeks to several months after picking, so store pears in a cool place, checking regularly for ripening. When beginning to ripen, the skin will yellow slightly and at this point bring them into the house to ripen fully.

PECANS

Carya illinoinensis. Deciduous tree.

A gorgeous tree, worth growing for its shape and leaves alone, but with good varieties, in a sheltered sunny spot, you might just get lucky and end up with delicious nuts. Don't expect much from them for a few years; mine refused to grow above ground while they sent down sturdy roots, but finally, they woke up and sprang into life, and have at least tried to catch up. I've planted mine on a high spot by the river – they originate in the river basins of the southern states of America, and they seem to like the similar conditions.

VARIETIES: For the UK and other northerly climates, your chosen varieties should be a northern type pecan, which are early-producing trees. Try 'Campbell NC4', 'Carlson 3', 'Lucas' or 'Mullahy'. Self-fertile.

STARTING OFF: Source grafted trees from a specialist supplier.

POSITION: Full sun in a sheltered place with a rich, deep but well-draining soil.

SPACING: 6–7m apart.

PRODUCTIVITY/EFFICIENCY: Pecans need a good amount of sun

to fruit and are unlikely to fruit every year without it, but they require little of your time.

GROWING: Keep weed free around the base whilst the pecan is establishing its deep taproot in the first few years – it will appear not to grow during this time.

POTENTIAL PROBLEMS: Generally pest and disease free.

HARVEST: When the husks of the nuts start to split, spread a sheet on the ground under the pecan and shake its branches.

PINEAPPLE GUAVA

Acca sellowiana. Also known as: feijoa. Evergreen shrub.

A gorgeous shrub, rather like a larger-leaved olive, and with one of the most beautiful of the edible flowers, and with a flavour to match - fruity, crisp, sweet and with a spicy, slightly cinnamon hint, they are superb raw. In the warmest, most sheltered spots, ideally under cover, you might coax fruit from a pineapple guava too. The fruit looks like a small avocado and tastes somewhere between a pineapple and strawberry, which should be invitation enough to grow them if you have a sunny spot.

VARIETIES: Plenty of named varieties available, including 'Mammoth' and 'Triumph', though 'Smith' is supposed to be most likely to fruit in cooler climates. Check whether the variety you are buying is self-fertile or requires a pollinator, but again this is only necessary if you are hoping for fruit – they will produce edible flowers regardless.

STARTING OFF: Source plants from a specialist supplier.

POSITION: Tolerant of most situations, but prefers humus-rich and well-drained soil. Prefers full sun but will tolerate a little shade. If you are hoping for fruit give it the warmest spot you can – a walled garden is ideal. Pineapple guava is hardy to –12°C and suitable for the warmer parts of the UK.

SPACING: Pineapple guava can reach 2.5m in height and spread, but is easily kept smaller by pruning.

PRODUCTIVITY/EFFICIENCY: An attractive addition to your garden, but quite a large one for the return in edible flowers that you'll get. That said, it requires no maintenance.

GROWING: Prune as and if you fancy to keep this to a size you want.

POTENTIAL PROBLEMS: Generally pest and disease free.

HARVEST: Pick flowers throughout July. Pick fruit before the frosts set in – they may not yet be ripe but will ripen in storage.

PLUMS, DAMSONS AND GAGES

Prunus domestica and *Prunus insititia*. Deciduous tree.

Each of these three variations on a theme is very much worth considering. Although damsons tend to be more for cooking than eating fresh, variety plays a huge part – the 'Dittisham Damson' tree gives us incredibly juicy, succulent fruit that we eat fresh as much as cooked. There's such variation in flavour, texture and harvest time, that it's hard to generalise - better to spend time looking at specialist nursery catalogues, and picking the flavours and textures that take your fancy.

VARIETIES: Plums and gages are from the *Prunus domestica* species and damsons from *P. insititia*. Try 'Czar' for an early plum, 'Merryweather' for a heavy-cropping, late-ripening damson, or 'Early Transparent' for a sweet gage.

This group of plants can be self-sterile (needing a pollinator), partially self-fertile or self-fertile, so check whether a pollinator is needed when choosing your varieties, making sure pollination groups are compatible.

STARTING OFF: Source grafted plants from a good supplier.

POSITION: There are rootstocks available to suit most soil types. Although very hardy plums and gages are late-flowering, site in a frost-free place and the sunnier the better for dessert varieties, especially the later-ripening ones.

SPACING: 2.5–7m apart.

PRODUCTIVITY/EFFICIENCY: Plums, damsons and gages begin to fruit in 2–6 years, giving between 15–65kg of fruit, depending on rootstock.

GROWING: Plums, gages and damsons can easily be grown as pyramids, cordons or fans. Once the shape is established, you only need to remove dead and diseased wood each year. Thin fruits to 8cm. Mulch annually with compost or manure.

POTENTIAL PROBLEMS: Prune between May and October to avoid silver leaf. Choose varieties with some resistance to canker, such as 'Marjorie's Seedling' plum and 'Oullins Gage'.

HARVEST: Pick when fully coloured and the fruit comes away easily.

QUINCE

Cydonia oblonga. Deciduous tree.

Now that quinces are available as very dwarfing trees – growing to 1.5m or so in height and spread – there's almost no excuse for not growing one. Beautiful twisted white/pink blossom in spring, aromatic fruit in autumn and a lazily irregular habit all year round, quinces are right up there on my list of garden trees, whether you have an acre or a balcony. Let the fruit develop on the tree into autumn – perhaps even longer than the leaves cling to the tree – then pick and bring inside. The aroma will slowly build until it fills the room, perhaps even the house. Cooking brings out their loveliness; try a slice or two in an apple pie, poach them in cider or wine then bake them with butter, dried fruit and honey, or make membrillo – a semi-firm 'cheese', which is in fact a thick, sweet paste, that goes beautifully with meats and blue cheese.

VARIETIES: I've never been able to detect a difference in flavour between varieties, but if you are in a wet location, try 'Serbian Gold' (aka 'Lezovacz') or 'Champion', which have good blight resistance. Self-fertile.

STARTING OFF: Source grafted plants of named varieties from a fruit supplier.

POSITION: A sunny, sheltered position for best fruiting. Tolerant of most soils with the right rootstock.

SPACING: 4–5m apart, depending on rootstock; 1.5m if growing the very dwarf trees.

PRODUCTIVITY/EFFICIENCY: Quince will begin fruiting between years 2–4, depending on rootstock, and will yield around 15kg of fruit.

GROWING: An annual mulch of compost or manure will be appreciated. No pruning needed.

POTENTIAL PROBLEMS: Use resistant varieties to avoid leaf blight; incinerate fallen/affected leaves and prune and incinerate dead shoots in winter.

HARVEST: Pick in October as the fruits begin to soften. They can keep for 2 months or more if stored in a cool place.

RASPBERRIES

Rubus idaeus. Deciduous shrub.

If you put a gun to my head and made me choose between raspberries and strawberries, raspberries it would be. Their depth of flavour, that winey edge, just wins for me. There are two types: summer fruiting and autumn fruiting. I grow mostly autumn varieties as they grow canes that produce fruit in the same year, so you can strim the lot to ground level every year and they'll come back to fruit the next; their longer time in the sun gives them a deeper flavour too. Summer varieties can be very good indeed, but they fruit on canes that grew last year, which means pruning out only the canes that have fruited and leaving the rest for next year; plus they fruit when there are plenty of strawberries around.

VARIETIES: Try heavy-cropping 'Glen Clova' for tasty early fruit or 'Glen Magna' for late-season fruits. 'Tulameen' is a vigorous mid- to late-season raspberry with good flavour. Good autumn varieties to try are 'Autumn Bliss' and the yellow 'All Gold'. Self-fertile.

STARTING OFF: Source canes from a good fruit nursery.

POSITION: Full sun or a little shade. A fertile soil with good drainage is best. They will be shorter-lived on alkaline soils and don't thrive at all on chalk.

SPACING: Space summer raspberries 35–45cm apart in double rows 1m apart. Space autumn raspberries at 50cm apart and allow them to expand into a single narrow line about 30cm across.

PRODUCTIVITY/EFFICIENCY: Plants will supply you with a steady crop of berries over several weeks. With the right choice of cultivar you can harvest raspberries from June to November. Raspberry plants tend to live for around a dozen years.

GROWING: Support all this season's growth of summer raspberries, as this will provide fruit the following year. In autumn, remove fruited wood that was tied in the previous winter. Reduce amount of new stems to around 10 per metre, taking out the weakest first.

Autumn raspberries fruit on this year's growth and will usually be happy unsupported. Cut stems of autumn raspberries to the ground in late winter. Feed plants with an annual mulch of compost or manure.

POTENTIAL PROBLEMS: Don't plant where raspberries, blackberries or strawberries have previously been grown to limit the opportunities for diseases. You may need to net against birds. Cultivate the soil at the base of raspberries during the winter to deter raspberry beetle.

HARVEST: When ripe, raspberries readily come away from the plug.

RED- AND WHITE CURRANTS

Ribes rubrum. Deciduous shrub.

In many ways these two currants are under-appreciated, largely because of our love for sugar perhaps. Neither is the sweetest fruit, but both have a fine flavour and will produce well in less than the sunniest locations – fans are perfectly happy against a north-facing wall. Both make fabulous jelly to go with meat and cheese, and add a little delicious tartness to pies, tarts and crumbles.

VARIETIES: 'Jonkers van Tets' (aka 'Jonkheer van Tets') is an old early-cropping redcurrant, 'Red Lake' is mid-season and 'Rovada' is late season. 'White Versailles' and White Grape' are flavoursome white currants. Self-fertile.

STARTING OFF: Source plants from a fruit nursery or propagate from hardwood cuttings in winter.

POSITION: Tolerant of most soils and will fruit well in a fair amount of shade.

SPACING: 1.2–1.5m apart if growing as bushes, around 45cm for cordons and 2m for fans.

PRODUCTIVITY/EFFICIENCY: Red- and white currants will start to fruit in their second year, and will get to full production in around 6 years. They can fruit well for 20 years, producing around 4kg each year, and are happy in semi-shade where little other fruit thrives.

GROWING: Give an annual mulch of compost or manure. Formative prune main branches in winter and prune side shoots in summer.

POTENTIAL PROBLEMS: Summer pruning of side shoots to five leaves will help control blister aphid. Pick off any sawfly larvae in the spring to prevent defoliation. Net against birds.

HARVEST: Leave redcurrants for a few days after they have turned a lively red, in order to develop their sweetness. White currants will turn a creamy colour when ripe. Pinch whole trusses of fruit from the bush and use a fork to separate berries from the stalks.

RHUBARB

Rheum x *hybridum*. Hardy perennial.

One of my favourite flavours, and definitely one of the most reliable and easy to grow. Once established, expect rhubarb's huge leaves to push out early and strongly every spring – it's the delicious, fibrous, sour stalks at their centre you're after. I can't have enough of them, so I grow varieties that produce in succession and force some early. Forcing is as easy as putting a bucket (or traditional forcing pot) over an early variety and allowing the warm microclimate to hurry growth along. In the absence of light, the plant uses stored starches (rather than photosynthesis) to drive growth – some of these starches are converted into sugars in the process, resulting in pink, sweet stalks, a few weeks earlier than the first of the non-forced varieties.

VARIETIES: Try 'Timperley Early', which is one of the earliest rhubarbs, and 'Victoria', one of the latest. 'Holstein Blood Red' is an old variety with very red stems. You could try Himalayan rhubarb (*Rheum australe*) if you have the room. It is majestic and will provide you with large apple-flavoured stems when traditional rhubarb has gone over.

STARTING OFF: Source crowns from a good supplier or propagate by division in early spring, and plant whilst dormant (normally November to March). Plant with the crown at soil level, or just above if soil is on the wet side.

POSITION: Likes a humus-rich moist soil in full sun.

SPACING: 1m apart with 2m between rows, with 2m apart for Himalayan rhubarb.

PRODUCTIVITY/EFFICIENCY: Rhubarb can produce a steady supply of stems from April (earlier if forcing) to July if you choose varieties that crop in succession, and with very little input from you.

GROWING: Allow the plant to establish for a year before harvesting. Give plants an annual mulch with compost or preferably manure. Cut off flower stalks as they detract from edible stem production. Divide plants every 5 years or so to maintain vigour. For an early crop in January, force plants by covering with an upturned pot (holes covered), bucket or forcer, surrounded by fresh manure or straw if you have any. Leave forced plants to recover for the rest of the growing season and don't force the following year – they will be sufficiently recovered to force again the year after that.

POTENTIAL PROBLEMS: Generally pest and disease free.

HARVEST: Choose stems with good colour and leaves that have just opened, and, holding near the base, pull and twist. The leaves are poisonous so put them straight on the compost heap.

SCHISANDRA

Schisandra chinensis. Also known as: magnolia vine and five flavour berry. Deciduous vine.

I confess, I've not had much joy in getting Schisandra to fruit, but this may be ineptitude on my part: others I know find it no problem. It is a beautiful enough climber as it is, so I shall excuse its lack of productivity and pair it up with another variety in the hope that they pollinate each other and fruit a little better. The fruit hang in long racemes - strings of fruit - which look not unlike opaque redcurrants. They have a complex flavour that dominates the commercially available drink Amé; their Chinese name is wu wei zi, meaning 'fruit of five flavours'.

VARIETIES: Schisandra plants are either male or female, and both are required for pollination. However, you could try 'Eastern Prince', which is self-fertile.

STARTING OFF: Source plants from a specialist supplier or propagate established plants by division.

POSITION: A moist and preferably acid soil, although, with lots of organic matter dug in, it will grow in a more alkaline soil. Will tolerate some shade.

SPACING: Can reach 7m in height.

PRODUCTIVITY/EFFICIENCY: Given some support this vine can be left largely to its own devices, though it will take a few years for fruiting to begin.

GROWING: Prune in spring to reduce size if you fancy. Plants need support but this could be the canopy of a tree.

POTENTIAL PROBLEMS: Generally pest and disease free.

HARVEST: Pick the fruit in autumn when berries are bright red.

SEA BUCKTHORN

Hippophae species. Deciduous shrub.

A rough, tough, hardy shrub, which you may find naturalised in sand dunes in parts of the UK. An excellent hedging plant if keeping people or animals out/in is your aim. The fruit are rich in vitamins A and C, and abundantly borne, but might generously be described as astringent. Let this not dissuade you from investigating their loveliness - sea buckthorn's flavour is quite unique and hard to navigate via other fruit, almost more of a flavoursome aroma - but sweetened in drinks or cocktails is quite something, and sea buckthorn makes one of the most delicious ice creams I've ever eaten.

VARIETIES: There are several sea buckthorn species, but the most edible are *H. rhamnoides* and *H. salicifolia*. You will need both male and female plants for pollination.

STARTING OFF: Source plants from a specialist supplier.

POSITION: Well-drained soil in full sun. Sea buckthorns are tolerant of exposure.

SPACING: Space 5–8m apart, depending on variety. If planting as a hedge, space at around 1m.

PRODUCTIVITY/EFFICIENCY: Heavy crops of fruit are borne from the third year. An excellent hedging plant, ground stabiliser and bee plant.

GROWING: Cut off any suckers that appear where you don't want them.

POTENTIAL PROBLEMS: Generally pest and disease free.

HARVEST: Snip the fruit from the plant when the berries become a rich orange and soften slightly to the touch. This will be in September and October.

STRAWBERRIES

Fragaria x *ananassa*. Hardy perennial.

If you can, find room for a few strawberries – even if just in a container. The flavours of the best homegrown varieties are such a league apart from those in the shops and, as is usually the case, you'll find the difference it makes is huge to pick them when fully ripe. Unless you are a keen preserver, I'd suggest having plants that ripen at different times, to give you a successional harvest rather than a glut. I eat most of my strawberries fresh, either straight from the plant or in Eton mess, knickerbocker glories and other summery desserts. Their flavour transfers well into most preserves – jams and fruit leather especially – and strawberry ice cream is so much better when made with home grown.

VARIETIES: There is a multitude to choose from, but it's possible to be in strawberries from May right through to November. Try 'Honeoye', 'Cambridge Favourite', 'Royal Sovereign' and 'Mara des Bois', along with 'everbearing' varieties such as 'Flamenco' and 'Albion' for the latest strawberries. You could also try alpine strawberries such as 'Mignonette' (see page 116). Self-fertile.

STARTING OFF: Usually available as barefoot mini-plants or in pots – they can be planted whenever they are available, but ideally in late summer/early autumn when the ground is still warm. You can also propagate them from runners.

POSITION: Full sun in moisture-retentive, well-drained soil.

SPACING: Plant strawberries 50cm apart in rows with 90cm between rows.

PRODUCTIVITY/EFFICIENCY: Plants usually produce well and with the right choice of varieties can give a long season of fruit, but not without some input: manure as a feed and straw as a mulch around the plants help give a continued high harvest. Plants tend to tire after around 5 years, so replant a quarter every year after year 5.

GROWING: Suppress weeds and keep soil moist by mulching between the rows with straw when you see the first fruits are appearing. When fruiting is over, cut back the fruited stems, runners and leaves and add well-rotted manure or compost.

POTENTIAL PROBLEMS: Net against birds who want your strawberries as much as you do. Slugs and snails can be a problem in a wet year as can botrytis. Use your preferred method on the former and take care not to splash your strawberries when watering, and to keep a good airflow around plants to avoid the latter.

HARVEST: Pick when well coloured and when the sun is warm to bring out their fullest flavour.

SWEET CHESTNUTS

Castanea species. Deciduous tree.

A few years ago I turned a corner with sweet chestnuts. As with many things, pairing them with cream and chocolate brought out the best in them (they'd probably make my shoe taste good too), and as a cake, it's hard to better. Roasted over an open fire, as in the old festive song, they are fabulously nutty and sweet –

but be careful not to burn them, as they turn bitter very easily. Easy to grow, increasingly reliable producers as climate change takes effect, and relatively untroubled by pests and diseases, sweet chestnuts are a fine choice for a good-sized garden or larger.

VARIETIES: Sweet chestnuts are from the *Castanea sativa* species, or are a hybrid *C. sativa* x *C. crenata*. 'Bouche de Betizac' and 'Marigoule' are hybrids that are doing well in the UK. *C. sativa* 'Belle Epine' is a good pollinator and fruiter. Generally, sweet chestnuts are not self-fertile and will need another variety to pollinate, and although some such as 'Marigoule' are partially self-fertile, they will still produce more with a pollinator.

STARTING OFF: Source grafted plants from a specialist supplier.

POSITION: A sunny spot in well-drained soil that ranges from acid to neutral.

SPACING: A full-grown tree can reach 20m high and 15m wide; however, size can be controlled by pruning or coppicing, in which case plant at around 8m apart.

PRODUCTIVITY/EFFICIENCY: A 50kg harvest of chestnuts from a 10-year-old tree is not unusual.

GROWING: If restricting the size of your chestnuts, prune lightly in winter into an open goblet shape during the first 2 or 3 years after planting, or coppice every 10 years or so. Coppiced trees will take 2 or 3 years to begin producing nuts again. If growing as a standard tree little is required.

POTENTIAL PROBLEMS: Use sticky or pheromone traps if chestnut weevil or chestnut codling moths are troublesome, although in reality damage is rarely significant from these pests.

HARVEST: Chestnuts fall to the ground when ready and at the same time as the leaves. They tend to fall over a period of 2 weeks, and will need collecting every other day or so to prevent deteriorating. A nut wizard makes collecting a great deal easier. Nuts will store for a few weeks if allowed to dry in the sun or at room temperature for a couple of days, and are then stored in the fridge. They also freeze well after boiling for 5 minutes and then peeling. They will keep for several years if dehydrated.

WALNUTS

Juglans regia. Deciduous tree.

As with sweet chestnuts, climate change means that walnuts are likely to be ever more prolific and reliable croppers in the UK, and if you have a bit of space, they make a fine tree. Or rather trees, as while many varieties are self-fertile, they'll produce bigger crops more reliably with a pollinating partner. Growing your own means you get the tastiest varieties and the chance to pick green walnuts – harvested before the shell forms – which make a fabulous aperitif and are delicious pickled. We eat most of our walnuts fresh, often with cheese and fruit, occasionally in chicken recipes, and in endless puddings.

VARIETIES: For the UK, use late-flowering varieties that will side-step any frosts. 'Franquette' and 'Broadview' are both late flowering as well as good quality, early yielding and disease resistant. You could also try 'Corne du Perigord' and 'Fernor', which are also disease resistant. Check with your supplier whether your chosen variety requires a pollinator.

STARTING OFF: Source grafted plants from a good supplier. There are rootstocks to suit most soil types so ask your supplier.

POSITION: Tolerant of most soils but full sun is a must.

SPACING: A full-size tree can reach 20m high and 15m wide, although pruning can keep that to 8 metres or so wide.

PRODUCTIVITY/EFFICIENCY: Grafted trees can start cropping in 3–4 years, but will take around 10 years or so to produce large quantities.

GROWING: Prune lightly in winter into an open goblet shape during the first few years after planting. Thereafter, remove dead or crossing branches and prune to restrict size. Don't plant anything valuable underneath as walnuts can release chemicals that inhibit the growth of neighbours.

POTENTIAL PROBLEMS: Grow blight-resistant varieties to avoid leaf spot and walnut blight. Some plants, such as apples, will not grow well next to walnut trees. Trap and (as is required by law) humanely kill squirrels by whichever method you find best if you don't want to share your nuts.

HARVEST: Pick walnuts green for pickling in midsummer, with the main harvest in autumn.

WORCESTERBERRIES

Ribes divaricatum. Hardy shrub.

Worcesterberries are a thorny North American relative of the gooseberry, with a touch of blackberry about them in looks and flavour. What you gain in disease resistance and productivity, you pay for a little in thorns, but the flavour is very much worth it – like a slightly blackcurranty gooseberry, that was for some time thought to be a cross between the two.

VARIETIES: Usually found only in its generic form.

STARTING OFF: Source bare-root or pot-grown plants from a good supplier, or propagate from hardwood cuttings in autumn.

POSITION: Moist, fertile but well-drained soil. These berries will also do well on a poor soil, as long as it's not wet.

SPACING: 1.8m apart.

PRODUCTIVITY/EFFICIENCY: A very productive fruit bush.

GROWING: Prune as for gooseberries to keep to the size you prefer.

POTENTIAL PROBLEMS: Worcesterberries avoid most of the diseases that afflict blackcurrants and gooseberries, although birds can be a problem. Prune the centre of the plant to be light and airy to deter sawfly.

HARVEST: Pick berries in late July/early August when a deep black colour and just softening to the touch.

HERBS AND SPICES

ANGELICA

Angelica archangelica. Also known as: Garden Angelica, Holy Ghost and Norwegian Angelica. Hardy biennial.

A lovely umbelliferous herb, tall and striking. Not one you'll use every day in all likelihood, but its looks may bump it up the pecking order above some others, perhaps. Its flavour is gently astringent, musky even, being one of the key ingredients in many gins. Really worthwhile investigating.

VARIETIES: There are many ornamental angelicas available, but the edible type is the ecclesiastically named *Angelica archangelica.*

STARTING OFF: Sow fresh seeds in early autumn in modules for planting out in mid-spring, or, alternatively, sow direct where they are to grow. Seeds will lose their viability quickly so do not save from one year to the next.

POSITION: Prefers at least partial shade and can do very well in deep shade. Likes a moist soil.

SPACING: 1.2m apart.

PRODUCTIVITY/EFFICIENCY: As trouble free and low maintenance as it gets, happy in shade and great looking.

GROWING: Angelica is a biennial and will die after flowering, but self-seeds freely.

POTENTIAL PROBLEMS: Slugs and snails can attack young plants.

HARVEST: Cut young leaves and stalks for crystallising in early summer. Seeds are ready to harvest from summer onwards.

ANISE HYSSOP

Agastache foeniculum. Also known as: liquorice mint. Hardy perennial.

A beautiful, aromatic and delicious herb that, I confess, I grow as much for its looks and bee-friendliness as its fine flavour. It resembles an elegant mint, producing striking purple bottle-brush flowers in summer. The leaves and flowers taste of mint and aniseed in an approximately 1:3 ratio, and has that gentle sweetening effect that sweet cicely's aniseed also brings. Use the leaves or flowers raw – more than a moment's cooking robs its flavour. Try them shredded finely with strawberries, in cocktails, or with seafood.

VARIETIES: Named varieties are hard to find.

STARTING OFF: Source plants from a specialist supplier or grow from seed under cover in spring.

POSITION: A sunny spot in well-drained and rich soil. Can be grown in a large container.

SPACING: 30–45cm apart. Can reach 1m in height.

PRODUCTIVITY/EFFICIENCY: Fresh leaves are produced throughout the growing season. It may be worth growing two plants if you want both leaves and flowers – the leaves become tougher once the plant starts to flower.

GROWING: Pick off flower heads if you want to prolong your supply of tender leaves.

POTENTIAL PROBLEMS: As with most herbs, relatively untroubled by pests and diseases.

HARVEST: Pick tender leaves and flower heads through summer as needed. Any flowers left to seed and desiccate can be picked off through winter to add their distinctive flavour to sorbets, syrups and ice creams.

BABINGTON'S LEEK

Allium ampeloprasum var. *babingtonii*. A hardy, native perennial.

A fine perennial leek that would be welcome at any time of year, but flourishing as it does in the back end of winter and into spring it is all the more valuable. When everything else is shutting down, Babington's leek wakes up, being ready to harvest as the first hint of spring is in the air. Sweeter than regular leeks, and with a warm gentle hint of garlic, I like them best cut just above the base as mini leeks. Any that you don't pick do as leeks do: throw up long stems, which develop glorious seed heads. Bees love them, as do I – the florets add oniony bite scattered over salads and on pizzas.

VARIETIES: No named varieties.

STARTING OFF: Source bulbils from a good supplier and either grow on in a 1 litre pot for planting out later, or sow direct. Can be dug up, split and divided to create new plants.

POSITION: Very unfussy, and being native to our seashores is hardy and robust.

SPACING: 45cm or so apart.

PRODUCTIVITY/EFFICIENCY: A very low-maintenance plant that gives three different crops at different times of year, particularly valuable for its leeks in late winter and early spring.

GROWING: Little maintenance needed. The plant will clump up over the years if allowed, and gently self-sow.

POTENTIAL PROBLEMS: Generally pest and disease free.

HARVEST: Harvest the bulbs in late summer (these can be stored if dried like regular onions), replanting one or two for future crops. Bulbils can also be used but make sure you get them before they have formed a papery skin. During the winter, cut the stems at ground level and use as you would leeks.

BASIL

Ocimum basilicum. Half-hardy annual.

The herb almost everybody loves, that eaten with a sun-warm tomato straight from the vine sums up summer in a mouthful. Easy to grow, prolific and expensive to buy in the shops, basil is one of the great transformers – sweet, bright and with an aniseed/liquorice flavour that even those who profess to dislike aniseed or liquorice seem to love. As well as pairing it with tomatoes and mozzarella, basil works beautifully with chicken and in ice cream (honestly). As with many annual herbs, use it raw: its flavour and aroma vanish when cooked.

VARIETIES: Try the classic 'Sweet Genovese' or 'Lettuce Leaf' with its large crinkly leaves. 'Siam Queen' has an intense liquorice flavour and aroma, with a lovely lemony edge which makes it good for Asian dishes. The bushy 'Greek' basil with its tiny leaves is a must on the window sill and perhaps my favourite for scattering through salads. Do also try 'Cinnamon' basil and 'Lime' basil.

STARTING OFF: Sow seed in modules under cover from late spring until August, planting out once the danger of frosts has passed. Make successional sowings for continuous supply throughout the summer.

POSITION: A sunny spot in rich and moist but free-draining soil. Basil will grow happily in pots but don't let it dry out.

SPACING: 15–20cm apart.

PRODUCTIVITY/EFFICIENCY: A very effective transformer. A few basil plants can provide you with all you need throughout the summer.

GROWING: Thrives in warmth, so grow at least some under cover as insurance against a UK summer if you can. Pinch out the shoots to make a bushy plant and remove the flowers to keep the best flavour.

POTENTIAL PROBLEMS: Generally pest and disease free but doesn't like cold temperatures.

HARVEST: In the height of summer, pick off individual leaves as needed – take care, as they bruise easily.

BAY

Laurus nobilis. Evergreen shrub/tree.

I'm not sure if I've had a piece of fish or a stew where bay hasn't been involved since about 1983. It has a little of so much going on, both dark and light: citrus, smoky fires, rich roses and, peculiarly, more than a hint of cola bottles, those rubbery sweets of my childhood. Give it a sheltered, sunny spot and you'll have years of sweet-savoury brightness and depth at your fingertips.

As well as fish, soups and stews, bay and dairy is a match made in heaven – bay ice cream is a must-try.

VARIETIES: There are few named cultivars but you could try 'Aurea' for yellow leaves.

STARTING OFF: Source plants from a good supplier. They can be bought as trained forms.

POSITION: Bay will be happiest out of cold winds and frost pockets. Find it a spot in sun or partial shade with free-draining soil. It will happily grow in a container.

SPACING: Bay can reach 6m in height and width, but can easily be pruned to fit within your chosen area.

PRODUCTIVITY/EFFICIENCY: A single plant will provide you with plentiful bay.

GROWING: Generally, little is required but don't allow young plants to dry out, although older ones are fairly drought tolerant.

POTENTIAL PROBLEMS: Rarely bothered by pests and diseases.

HARVEST: Pick leaves as needed throughout the year. Older plants in warmer areas might also produce berries – these can be used as a spice.

BERGAMOT

Monarda didyma. Also known as: bee balm, lad's love and mountain mint. Hardy perennial.

Not the bergamot that gives the citrus wham to Earl Grey tea, but a beautiful, pungent herb, somewhere at the rosemary-marjoram end of the spectrum. A bee-friendly plant that repels plenty of would-be garden nuisances, so making it a fine companion plant for pest-prone plants.

Its flavour is quite 'big' so use sparingly, at least at first. Treat it more as you might an annual herb, adding it very late to cooking or just as you're serving. It pairs particularly well with squash and sweet root veg.

VARIETIES: There are a lot of ornamental varieties available. Try 'Croftway Pink' or 'Cambridge Scarlet' if you're after different colour flowers. You could also try M. *citriodora* or 'Lemon Bergamot' whose leaves are strongly lemony.

STARTING OFF: Buy plants or sow seed in modules in the spring. Seed needs warmth to germinate well.

POSITION: A rich moist soil in sun or partial shade.

SPACING: 50cm apart. Can reach up to 90cm in height.

PRODUCTIVITY/EFFICIENCY: A single plant should satisfy your culinary needs.

GROWING: Mulch to retain moisture, and water in dry weather. May need support. Remove flowers to prolong harvesting. You could grow more than one plant to allow bees to forage on those you don't cut back. The plants will need lifting and dividing every 3 years or so to maintain vigour.

POTENTIAL PROBLEMS: Generally pest and disease free.

HARVEST: The best flavour is just before the plant flowers. Leaves, shoot tips and flowers are all edible – the flowers raw and the leaves and shoots raw or cooked.

BORAGE

Borago officinalis. Hardy annual.

An absolute must for any garden, borage's cucumber flavour carried in its young leaves and flowers is wonderful added to salads, cocktails or with fruit such as strawberries. One of the great bee-friendly plants for the garden too. Grow it once and you are likely to find it springing up randomly in subsequent years. Borage brings life and colour unexpectedly, self-sowing readily to lift otherwise green veg beds early in the season and through into late autumn.

VARIETIES: Borage is more usually seen in its blue form but the white *B. officinalis* 'Alba' is beautiful.

STARTING OFF: Seed germinates readily sown directly in April. Sow again around midsummer for a continual supply until the autumn.

POSITION: Full sun in most soils but prefers good drainage.

SPACING: 50cm apart and will reach 60–90cm in height.

PRODUCTIVITY/EFFICIENCY: You will have a continual supply of flowers from early summer (and earlier from self-sown plants) until October with little effort on your part. Plants self-seed happily.

GROWING: Taller plants may need staking. Deadhead to keep plants flowering.

POTENTIAL PROBLEMS: Generally pest and disease free.

HARVEST: Leaves and flowers are edible. If using leaves raw then pick them young.

CARAWAY

Carum carvi. Hardy biennial, often grown as an annual.

As with fennel seed, caraway is more of a spice than a herb. Looking somewhere between a fern and a herb fennel plant, I never use the leaves of caraway (though some do as a breath freshener or in place of parsley), but the seeds are a real treat. I use them with brassicas, cabbages especially, and a handful in bread dough brings a lovely nuttiness to the cooked loaf. Try caraway with fruit too: they bring a kind of mouth-freshness like freshly brushed teeth on a cold morning.

VARIETIES: Most often sold in its generic form.

STARTING OFF: The seed needs warmth to germinate, so sow seed under cover in modules in April, or direct from May to July.

POSITION: Full sun or partial shade in a moisture-retentive soil with good drainage.

SPACING: 25cm apart.

PRODUCTIVITY/EFFICIENCY: Plants will flower the year after they are sown and will occupy the ground for some time. Just a few plants will provide you with a reasonable amount of seed and may self-sow if allowed to.

GROWING: A very deep-rooting plant that doesn't like being transplanted.

POTENTIAL PROBLEMS: Generally pest and disease free.

HARVEST: Pick fresh leaves as required. If harvesting the seed then cut plant stems a few centimetres above the ground in the middle of a warm sunny day and when the heads are quite dry. Put the heads inside a paper bag and hang them upside down for a couple of weeks, after which the seed should be dry and come away easily from the plant.

CAROLINA ALLSPICE

Calycanthus floridus. Also known as: spicebush and sweet shrub. Deciduous shrub.

A beautiful, substantial shrub with the most heady, heavily perfumed flowers I grow, but it's the woody bark that makes it to the kitchen. Dried in the sun or in a low oven, the bark can be pounded or ground into a powder that has a flavour and aroma similar to cinnamon (which won't grow in this country). Use it as you would cinnamon, with fruit, in spice blends for pork, or dust it over porridge or rice pudding. Don't eat anything but the bark: the fruit and flowers are toxic.

VARIETIES: The variety 'Athens' is reputedly particularly fragrant. You could also try *C. occidentalis,* known as California allspice.

STARTING OFF: Source plants from a specialist nursery.

POSITION: Tolerant of most soils and in full sun for the best fragrance.

SPACING: Can reach 3m high and wide if allowed.

PRODUCTIVITY/EFFICIENCY: You will have to wait a year or two until the plant is well established before harvesting any branches, but thereafter it should provide you with all the spice you need and with little effort on your part.

GROWING: Prune to restrict size if need be whenever you wish, otherwise little maintenance required.

POTENTIAL PROBLEMS: Generally pest and disease free.

HARVEST: Cut out the drier-looking branches (which are usually stronger in taste) in July and August, peeling off the bark and drying on a window sill for storage.

CELERY LEAF

Apium graveolens var. *dulce.* Hardy biennial, mostly grown as an annual.

A close cousin of celery and celeriac, you can consider this a cut-and-come-again version of the former, ideal for adding a leafy end to soups and stews. I'm not a fan of raw celery, so am inclined to grow and use more of this. It's not a million flavour miles from lovage, but is altogether gentler; a few thinly sliced leaves in a leafy salad is far from overpowering. The leaves and seeds pair up equally well with apple and cheese.

VARIETIES: No named varieties available.

STARTING OFF: The seed is very small and easiest sown in trays and pricked out into modules. Sow under cover in early spring but don't cover the seed. Plant out as the soil warms up or direct sow when the soil is warm enough.

POSITION: A humus-rich, moist soil is preferred, as is some shade. Does well in containers if given sufficient water.

SPACING: 25cm apart, or around 10cm if growing as cut-and-come-again.

PRODUCTIVITY/EFFICIENCY: Celery leaf will give you a celery flavour over a longer period of time and for much less trouble than celery.

GROWING: Water if in danger of drying out – it likes being a little damp at all times. Cut back flower stems if you want to prolong leaf harvest.

POTENTIAL PROBLEMS: Generally pest and disease free.

HARVEST: Use leaves and stems in the plant's first year – in a sheltered spot you may have these through the winter. You can harvest leaves and stems in the second year too, but the flower stems must be cut back. Harvest the seeds in autumn of the second year, cutting stems on a dry day and hanging them upside down in a paper bag for a couple of weeks. Seed can then be easily separated from the plant.

CHERVIL

Anthriscus cerefolium. Also known as: garden chervil and hedge parsley. Hardy annual.

A fabulous, yet subtle herb that everyone should grow. Imagine a gentle, delicate parsley in looks and flavour crossed with the faintest hint of aniseed and you'll have chervil. As well as being fine on its own (notably with eggs, fish, chicken and in salads), it has a wonderfully generous ability to catalyse other herbs, making the best of them while keeping in the background itself. Very popular around the Mediterranean, and given how easily it produces, there is little excuse for it not to be here too.

VARIETIES: No named varieties available.

STARTING OFF: Sow seed in quantity, successively from March until autumn. Start early sowings in modules or guttering under cover. Later sowings can be made direct.

POSITION: Humus-rich, moisture-retentive soil in part-shade. Chervil does well in pots.

SPACING: 20cm apart.

PRODUCTIVITY/EFFICIENCY: Chervil can be harvested 6–8 weeks after sowing, can be cut several times and will provide you with leaves over the winter.

GROWING: Keep watered in dry weather. Chervil doesn't like being transplanted, so don't be surprised if you have a few losses if not sowing direct.

POTENTIAL PROBLEMS: Chervil will quickly run to seed if too hot or if the soil dries out.

HARVEST: Cut leaves 2–3cm above the soil and it will regrow. Harvesting is possible throughout the year, even in the depths of winter if under cover.

CHIVES

Allium schoenoprasum. Hardy perennial.

From early in February, when the narrow tubular leaves begin to spear out of the soil, until late autumn when they retreat from the cold, chives will feature in at least one meal most days. There's very little that intense onion zap won't improve – salads, cocktails, soups, pâtés and sauces to name just a few. The flowers, too, are as delicious as they are beautiful, broken over anything from leafy salads to hearty stews to add spots of onion flavour. Easy to grow, nearly impossible to accidentally kill and productive for years, they're almost compulsory.

VARIETIES: Try the white form *A. schoenoprasum* var. *albiflorum.*

You could also try garlic chives (*A. tuberosum*) or Siberian chives (*A. nutans*).

STARTING OFF: Source chive plants from a good supplier or divide established clumps.

POSITION: Tolerant of most soils and situations, but prefer sun and a moist, rich soil. Chives will grow happily in containers.

SPACING: 20–30cm apart.

PRODUCTIVITY/EFFICIENCY: For little effort after planting you can crop chives from spring through to autumn, for years.

GROWING: Watering in dry weather will keep leaf production going and hold flowering back. Give an occasional mulch of compost.

POTENTIAL PROBLEMS: Generally pest and disease free.

HARVEST: Cut leaves near to the ground. Separate flower heads into florets for use in salads and garnishes.

CORIANDER

Coriandrum sativum. Hardy annual.

I treat coriander as two very distinct crops now: growing it as microleaves for the full intense coriander leaf flavour; and letting some plants develop to full size and go to seed (like anyone can stop them), letting them be their beautiful selves before collecting the seed. As micros, the flavour has everything you want from coriander – aromatic pungency and smooth intensity, with none of the cloying soapiness that can come with more mature leaves. Sow them densely.

VARIETIES: 'Santo' and 'Leisure' are reputedly slower to bolt than most, and 'Confetti' has very finely cut foliage and a particularly sweet flavour.

STARTING OFF: Doesn't like transplanting, so sow seed in modules or guttering under cover from early April (earlier if cropping under cover). Begin sowing direct from late April and sow successively through the summer. Coriander will do well in a pot and it works well as microleaves.

POSITION: A rich, moisture-retentive soil (but not wet) and some shade are preferable to delay plants running to seed.

SPACING: 20cm apart for regular coriander growing; 50cm for large plants to go to seed; densely for microleaves.

PRODUCTIVITY/EFFICIENCY: Coriander plants do run to seed quickly, but as the flowers and green seeds can also be eaten it is a very useful plant.

GROWING: Water in dry weather.

POTENTIAL PROBLEMS: Plants are quick to run to seed, but this can be slowed by watering in dry weather and frequently cutting the leaves back to 3cm or so above the ground.

HARVEST: Cut leaves to 3cm above soil level, pick flower heads and green seeds as desired. Seeds can also be allowed to dry on the plant. For micros, harvest (either by cutting or lifting from the compost) when just 5cm tall – a pinch of a dozen or so is all you need to brighten up salads or seafood, such is the seedlings' intensity.

D

DILL

Anethum graveolens. Hardy annual.

I have a bit of a love-hate relationship with dill: there's a threshold over which it shifts from a gorgeous, aromatic transformer of eggs, seafood and onions to borderline throat-catching and excessive – like smoke from a pinched candle. On the right side of the line, I love its ability to wake up a straight mayonnaise, bring cucumbers out of their shell, and lift potatoes and carrots in a completely different direction from other herbs.

VARIETIES: 'Super Dukat' reputedly has a finer flavour than the generic type.

STARTING OFF: Doesn't like transplanting so sow seed in modules from early April (earlier if cropping under cover). Begin sowing direct from late April and sow successively through the summer.

POSITION: Prefers a light soil with good drainage and some shade to hold back flowering.

SPACING: Around 30cm apart.

PRODUCTIVITY/EFFICIENCY: Easy to grow, dill will be ready to harvest in 6–8 weeks.

GROWING: Water in dry weather to stop plants running to seed and cut out any flower stems to keep leaf production going.

POTENTIAL PROBLEMS: Generally pest and disease free.

HARVEST: Cut leaves as required. If harvesting seed for storage, cut stems on a dry day and hang them upside down for 2 weeks with the heads in a paper bag. They can then be easily separated from the plant.

ENGLISH MACE

Achillea ageratum. Also known as: Sweet Nancy. Hardy perennial.

Not the mace often used to spice up curry recipes, but a tall leafy herb with creamy daisy-like flowers. The leaves carry a distinctive flavour and scent that is somewhere in the middle of mint and chamomile. It goes well with chicken and fish especially, and in soups and stews. Mild and fresh flavoured, I tend to use the leaves as a flavouring to infuse, as when chewed the flavour becomes stronger, leaving a slight (although not unpleasant) tingle on the tongue. A beautiful and distinctive herb.

VARIETIES: Generic.

STARTING OFF: Source plants from a specialist supplier or divide existing plants in the spring or autumn.

POSITION: Tolerant of most well-drained soils and in a sunny position.

SPACING: 30cm apart.

PRODUCTIVITY/EFFICIENCY: Leaves can be harvested throughout the growing season.

GROWING: Little maintenance is required, but cut back flower stems to promote fresh growth.

POTENTIAL PROBLEMS: Generally pest and disease free

HARVEST: Pick fresh young leaves throughout the growing season.

F

FENNEL

Foeniculum vulgare. Hardy annual.

Distinct from Florence fennel (grown for its bulb), though herb fennel does share some of its wonderful aniseed. The leaves (thin fronds, not unlike dill) are fabulous used sparingly to pep up a leafy salad, tomatoes and fish, with its sweet, fragrant aniseed, but it is the seeds that come in late summer that I love most. They make the finest of fudges, bring a fresh bright edge to bread and are one of the cornerstones of five spice. A reliable self-seeder, which once grown will pop up every year unless you pick all the seeds.

VARIETIES: There is a purple-leaved form, *F. vulgare* 'Purpureum', or try 'Giant Bronze'.

STARTING OFF: Source plants from a good supplier or can easily be grown from seed. Sow in modules in spring or autumn, planting out when 7–10cm tall.

POSITION: Tolerant of most soils with reasonable drainage but likes them moist and to be in the sun. Fennel has a big taproot and consequently is fairly resilient. It can be grown in a container, if the pot is deep enough.

SPACING: 50cm–1m apart. Plants can reach 2.5m in height.

PRODUCTIVITY/EFFICIENCY: Will come back year on year with no effort on your part, with edible leaves from early spring until autumn.

GROWING: Cut any flower stems back to the ground to encourage leafy growth and grow more than one if you want to harvest seeds as well as leaves. Replace plants every few years.

POTENTIAL PROBLEMS: Fennel seeds very freely, so cut back flower stems before seed is ripe if you want to limit its spread.

HARVEST: Cut leaves as desired. Harvest the seed any time, either when green for use fresh, or brown for further drying and storage.

FENUGREEK

Trigonella foenum-graecum. Half-hardy annual with some frost resistance.

With its gentle curry flavour, fenugreek lifts and warms salads and soups, and is easy to grow. I grow most of ours as micro-leaves or sprouts – the volume may be small but the flavour is intense and clean. It's also very good left to grow into larger plants and the leaves and seeds picked for the kitchen.

VARIETIES: Fenugreek is found in white- and yellow-flowered forms. The white-flowered form has slightly larger leaves and will not regrow after cutting. The yellow-flowered form is the hardier of the two and can be cut several times.

STARTING OFF: Fenugreek doesn't like being transplanted so sow direct between April and August, or grow as microleaves or sprouts by sowing reasonably thickly into a seed tray or guttering on your window sill.

POSITION: Full sun and good drainage.

SPACING: Sow in drills 20cm apart and thin to 5cm apart within the row. Alternatively, broadcast sparingly.

PRODUCTIVITY/EFFICIENCY: Leaves are ready to be harvested around 6 weeks from sowing. If you only want to make one sowing in the year then grow the yellow-flowered form, which will regrow after cutting. Fenugreek can also act as a green manure by fixing nitrogen in the soil.

GROWING: Cut back any flower stems to encourage fresh leafy growth.

POTENTIAL PROBLEMS: Generally pest and disease free.

HARVEST: Cut microleaves when they are 3–4cm tall, before they become bitter. Harvest fenugreek leaves when the plant is 25cm or so tall. If harvesting the seed, cut flower stems on a dry day when the pods are yellow and before they have split. Hang them upside down in a paper bag to dry for around 2 weeks.

FRENCH TARRAGON

Artemisia dracunculus. Half-hardy perennial.

Yet another bright and breezy herb with aniseed at its heart, yet manages to be very much its distinctive self. It's hard to conjure up a finer roast chicken recipe than one with French tarragon – they were born to be together. As a partner to chervil, parsley and chives it makes up *fines herbes* – a handful of which in an omelette is a fine lunch indeed. Tarragon mayo, vinegar and béarnaise sauce are, if you need them, three other fabulous reasons to grow this excellent herb. It is really trouble free when given heat, light and a well-drained soil.

VARIETIES: Sold in its generic form, but you could also try the annual Mexican tarragon. Russian tarragon (*A. dracunculus dracunculoides*) is hardy and can be grown from seed, but its flavour is inferior to French tarragon.

STARTING OFF: Source plants from a good supplier or propagate using runners from established plants.

POSITION: Full sun or partial shade in well-drained soil. French tarragon is particularly suited to a pot as you can move it inside when frosts and cold weather threaten.

SPACING: 45cm apart.

PRODUCTIVITY/EFFICIENCY: French tarragon can be harvested from late spring and through the summer months.

GROWING: Replace plants after a couple of years with younger ones propagated from runners, as tarragon loses its flavour with age.

POTENTIAL PROBLEMS: Generally pest and disease free.

HARVEST: Pick leaves and stems throughout the growing season.

HORSERADISH

Armoracia rusticana. Hardy perennial.

Like mint, nettles and willow, horseradish is pretty hard to kill off, making it a must-have if you are convinced that you have been born uniquely incapable of keeping any plant alive. The large upright leaves are not the prize here: the nose-twitching heat of its root is what you are after, and when it's so easy to grow, why not start your own supply? As a partner to beef it is unrivalled, used sparingly it adds punch to a dressing for coleslaw or greens and, heresy though it might be, I like it with cold lamb. Horseradish is one of those harvests that is so much better if grown yourself: the aroma (which complements the heat beautifully) fades quickly after grating, so ready-made sauces can never bridge the gap.

VARIETIES: Generic.

STARTING OFF: Source young plants from a good supplier and plant in spring or propagate from root cuttings in winter.

POSITION: Any moist soil will do, as horseradish is fairly indestructible. It can be grown in a container as long as it is deep.

SPACING: 45cm apart.

PRODUCTIVITY/EFFICIENCY: A no-maintenance flavouring for harvesting during the winter months.

GROWING: The flip side of its indestructibility is that its invasive nature is hard to combat. Either dig up what you don't need if it expands, or grow it in a container to limit spread. Water in dry weather while establishing.

POTENTIAL PROBLEMS: Generally pest and disease free.

HARVEST: Roots are very deep so break off the top 10–20cm. These will keep for a while in the fridge if wrapped in paper. Harvest liberally to check its spread. The leaves are also edible – hot when raw, mild when cooked. Try them shredded with bacon or in bubble and squeak.

HYSSOP

Hyssopus officinalis. Hardy perennial.

A gorgeous marriage of citrus and deep rosemary is carried in the leaves' flavour, complementing fish, red meat, cheese, soups and stews equally well. Don't let a garden nibble persuade you otherwise – it can (like lemon) seem rather too much when eaten raw, but when cooked, contrasting with salty dishes or softened by dairy ingredients, it comes into its own. It is also a beautiful plant for the garden, available in white-, blue- or pink-flowering versions.

VARIETIES: Generic.

STARTING OFF: Source young plants from a good supplier or start from seed in modules in spring.

POSITION: Likes a free-draining soil in full sun.

SPACING: 60cm apart, or 30cm if using as hedging.

PRODUCTIVITY/EFFICIENCY: A single plant will provide you with ample flavouring from spring to autumn.

GROWING: Deadheading flowers will encourage new leaves. Cut back hard in spring to promote new growth and a bushier plant. An occasional mulch of compost would be appreciated.

POTENTIAL PROBLEMS: Generally pest and disease free.

HARVEST: Pick leaves as required.

JAPANESE PARSLEY

Cryptotaenia japonica. Also known as: mitsuba. A perennial hardy to −10°C that can also be treated as an annual.

This clumpy perennial has leaves that resemble flat-leaved parsley and carry much of the same flavour, softened with celery and a hint of bright angelica. Use it where you might parsley, in Japanese recipes that call for mitsuba and try it with fish.

VARIETIES: Generic.

STARTING OFF: Sow seed in spring or autumn in modules under cover. Sow direct from April.

POSITION: Prefers moist soil and a shady place, turning yellow if grown in full sun.

SPACING: 20cm apart if using as ground cover; 10cm if growing as a cut-and-come-again crop.

PRODUCTIVITY/EFFICIENCY: Takes little space for a punchy harvest, and needs no attention to produce it.

GROWING: Little maintenance required.

POTENTIAL PROBLEMS: Protect young plants and new spring growth from slugs and snails.

HARVEST: Cut leaves and stems as desired throughout the growing season and lightly through the winter. The seeds carry a similar flavour and can be used fresh or dried.

LAVENDER

Lavandula species. Hardy evergreen perennial.

You don't need a reason beyond its looks and perfume to grow lavender, but used sparingly it is a wonderful thing to add to your palate of culinary herbs. It's certainly something that is easy to overdo, but a little used in custard, biscuits, ice cream or in place of rosemary with roast lamb shows it off at its best. Easy to grow, as long as it has full sun and a well-drained, sheltered spot.

VARIETIES: *Lavandula angustifolia* varieties are the best for culinary purposes. You could try 'Hidcote' for its intense blue colour, 'Alba' for white flowers or 'Munstead' for purple blooms. *Lavandula* x *intermedia* 'Provence' is also highly rated for its flavour.

STARTING OFF: Source plants of named varieties from a good supplier or grow *L. angustifolia* from seed in spring. You can also propagate, taking softwood cuttings in early summer or hardwood cuttings in autumn.

POSITION: Full sun in free-draining soil. Lavender is very happy in a container.

SPACING: 30–90cm apart depending on if you are growing as a low hedge or a single plant.

PRODUCTIVITY/EFFICIENCY: Plants provide plentiful leaves and flowers throughout the growing season, need little attention and have few potential problems. Do avoid damp spots though, as root rots can occur. Should rosemary beetle appear, shake them off and remove.

GROWING: Water whilst establishing. Trim to a neat domed shape in spring and cut back after flowering in August taking care not to cut back into old wood as new growth rarely springs from it.

POTENTIAL PROBLEMS: Generally pest and disease free.

HARVEST: Pick leaves and flowers as required. The flowers are at their best just before they open.

LEMON BALM

Melissa officinalis. Hardy perennial.

One I grew for its unspectacular loveliness covering the ground, drawing in insects and adding a soft green/yellow to the forest garden before discovering its fine partnership with mint in a herb tea. And I'm not a fan of most herb teas. If you want a lemony flavour for cooking, I'd look no further than lemon verbena or lemongrass, but neither of those flourishes when grown in most positions outside in Britain, while lemon balm gives you the option, and is a great all-rounder in the garden.

VARIETIES: You could try *M. officinalis* 'Aurea' or 'All Gold' for a yellow-leaved lemon balm. 'Quedlinburger Niederliegende' has a stronger flavour.

STARTING OFF: Grows easily from seed or divide established plants in spring or autumn.

POSITION: Relatively unfussy about soil type but likes decent drainage. Lemon balm is happy in sun or part-shade and will do very well in a container.

SPACING: 45cm apart.

PRODUCTIVITY/EFFICIENCY: A herb that will provide you with plentiful leaves throughout the growing season and with very little effort on your part.

POTENTIAL PROBLEMS: None.

GROWING: Cut back a proportion of the flowering stems to maintain a supply of flavoursome, young leaves and if you want to keep self-seeding to a minimum. Bees will appreciate it if you leave a few flower stems for them.

HARVEST: Fresh, young leaves throughout the growing season, or dry by gathering young stems just before flowering and laying them on a tray in the airing cupboard.

LEMONGRASS

Cymbopogon citratus. Tender perennial.

The sweet aromatic herb that lends its spicy lemon flavour and fragrance to so many of the Southeast Asian dishes we know.

Although the stems are increasingly available in the shops, growing lemongrass means you can use the leaves too. Both carry that bright, fresh lemon taste that works so well in fragrant curries, soups, and with fish, as well as when poaching fruit.

VARIETIES: Usually sold in its generic form.

STARTING OFF: Source plants from a specialist nursery or sow seed in modules in spring (it needs warmth to germinate), potting on when the roots are showing. You can also propagate by dividing established plants or you could even try rooting shop-bought lemongrass by putting in a glass of water.

POSITION: Lemongrass is most suitable for growing in a pot so that it can be brought indoors over the winter. It will appreciate as much heat as you can give it during the spring and summer but keep soil moist.

SPACING: 30cm apart.

PRODUCTIVITY/EFFICIENCY: Little effort required in return for fresh, flavoursome stems. Plants are ready to harvest from their first year.

GROWING: Ensure compost is kept moist especially during spring and autumn, and a monthly feed from spring into autumn will be appreciated.

POTENTIAL PROBLEMS: Generally pest and disease free.

HARVEST: Cut stems as required through summer. Younger leaves can also be used as a flavouring.

LEMON VERBENA

Aloysia triphylla (syn. *A. citriodora*). Half-hardy perennial.

Give me three herbs to take to a desert island and this would be one of them; limit me to just one, and it still might make it. It has everything you'd want from a lemon but with a uniquely sherbety fizz. Pam the Jam, of River Cottage fame, has a bedroom window-high plant growing against her house, protected from the worst of the winds and enjoying the heat reflected from the wall; it flourishes outside and I envy her every centimetre of it. For the rest of us, this is one to grow undercover or in a pot to bring indoors through the coldest months. The leaves are used as you might bay – for the infused flavouring rather than actually eating them. I use it most in cocktails (fruit and alcohol) and in ice creams, though in summer I'm inclined to put it in cakes, make a syrup of it (infuse a fistful of leaves with equal amounts of simmering water and sugar) and put it through a grinder with sugar to add bright zip. A must-have.

VARIETIES: Generic.

STARTING OFF: Source plants from a good supplier or propagate from softwood cuttings.

POSITION: Drainage and a bit of extra warmth are key for the survival of lemon verbena. Grow in a tunnel or at the base of a wall in a warm sheltered spot. Lemon verbena will do well in a container.

SPACING: Can reach 2.5m in height and width.

PRODUCTIVITY/EFFICIENCY: A true transformer, giving huge flavour from little volume. You can harvest leaves throughout the growing season and even pick desiccated leaves from the plant in winter. A great herb for container growing.

GROWING: Responds well to a good prune in spring. Bring under cover in winter as they can suffer if the temperatures drop low.

POTENTIAL PROBLEMS: Generally pest and disease free.

HARVEST: Pick fresh leaves as required from mid-spring into autumn.

LOVAGE

Levisticum officinale. Hardy perennial.

I can find no better way of describing lovage than how I always do: like the best vegetable stock, in leaf form. You don't need much - a leaf or two is usually plenty - which makes a joke of its size (see Spacing below). It's rather lovely in its green, leafy way - when established, it is visually a cross between rhubarb and flat-leaved parsley. Try the seeds late in the season too: they're similarly savoury and really good sparingly used in a loaf or in soups and stews.

VARIETIES: No named varieties available.

STARTING OFF: Source young plants from a good supplier or sow seed in modules in spring, planting out when a few centimetres tall. Plants can also be propagated by division in spring or autumn.

POSITION: Sun or partial shade in a moist soil with reasonable drainage.

SPACING: If growing more than one, space 1m or so apart. Left alone, lovage will reach 2m in height.

PRODUCTIVITY/EFFICIENCY: A little goes a long way with lovage and a single plant should provide you with plenty, with little required on your part.

GROWING: Cutting plants back hard in June will promote fresh new growth.

POTENTIAL PROBLEMS: Generally pest and disease free.

HARVEST: Pick leaves as required from early spring until early winter, with seeds ready in late summer and autumn.

MARIGOLD

Calendula officinalis. Also known as: pot marigold and common marigold. Hardy annual.

I'm not a huge fan of orange flowers but marigolds are an exception I can't help but make. Cheery without being gaudy, the bright flowers of the marigold break easily into their constituent narrow petals, which I use most to add a flourish to salads of all kinds. Their flavour is gentle – a faint pepperiness is all – but with their splash of colour, it's plenty. A handful of petals leach their orange readily when warmed through in olive oil, adding colour and a hint of pepper to dressings or in dishes such as paella. The leaves, while less striking, carry more of that peppery fresh flavour – superb in a leafy salad.

VARIETIES: Try 'Indian Prince' for purple-backed flowers and 'Sunset Buff' for a soft apricot-coloured flower.

STARTING OFF: Seed is quite big so sow in 9cm pots in spring or autumn, planting out when the roots are showing. Calendula is hardy and can also be sown direct outside where they are to flower.

POSITION: Likes a sunny spot but is quite unfussy about soil.

SPACING: 20cm or so apart.

PRODUCTIVITY/EFFICIENCY: As easy as anything. Not likely to be something you'll harvest frequently, but a sensory pleasure through the summer months and, once grown, it'll often seed itself year on year, saving you the trouble. A great companion plant, deterring asparagus beetle and drawing in aphid-eaters such as hoverflies.

GROWING: Water whilst establishing and deadhead to encourage more flowers to appear.

POTENTIAL PROBLEMS: Generally trouble free. Even slugs aren't that interested, though you may want to protect newly planted-out seedlings. If blackfly are bothersome wipe off or cut out affected parts.

HARVEST: Pick young tender leaves as needed through late spring and summer, and flowers when fully open. Keep them in water in the kitchen until you are ready for them.

MARJORAM AND OREGANO

Origanum majorana. Also known as: sweet marjoram and garden marjoram. Half-hardy perennial.

O. vulgare. Also known as: pot marjoram and wild marjoram. Hardy perennial.

Two of my favourite herbs, which, while distinct, are closely related and share a warm spiciness. Sweet marjoram is perhaps my favourite. It smells like the first evening I had in Corsica, a teenager's dream of the Mediterranean: hot, spicy and utterly exotic. While I treat sweet marjoram as I would a delicate herb such as chervil (using it to brighten tomato salads and so on, giving it no more than a moment's heat if that), oregano is altogether richer, weightier and adds savoury depth when cooked with beans, lamb, tomatoes or squash. That said, the smallest new leaves of either, cast sparingly into a salad or more generously strewn over a pizza before cooking, are hard to rival.

VARIETIES: You could also try O. *vulgare* 'Hot & Spicy' for a stronger flavour.

STARTING OFF: Source plants of both species from a good supplier or lift and divide established plants. If starting from seed, sow oregano in modules in spring or autumn, potting on once before planting out. Sow seed of sweet marjoram in spring.

POSITION: Likes a sheltered, warm, sunny spot in well-drained soil. The flavour will be more intense the dryer the conditions. Both species will do well in a pot. If growing sweet marjoram as a perennial, plant it somewhere very sheltered or in a pot that can be brought under cover over winter.

SPACING: 30cm apart.

PRODUCTIVITY/EFFICIENCY: Plentiful leaves from two or three plants over the growing season, with O. *vulgare* appearing year after year.

GROWING: Bring sweet marjoram pots inside over winter. Cut back flowering stems once they have gone over.

POTENTIAL PROBLEMS: Generally pest and disease free.

HARVEST: Harvest tender flower buds and leaves as required.

MINT

Mentha species. Hardy perennial.

I could write a book about mint. The varieties are too numerous and varied to do it justice in a few paragraphs, but I hope to stir up enough inquisitiveness that you investigate more than a standard garden mint, good as it may be. If you grow only one, make it Moroccan mint – it is the best for tea, and a fine all-rounder. Chocolate mint, too, makes a refreshingly different tea, a fine ice cream, and is my favourite for adding when poaching fruit (peaches, especially).

VARIETIES: Try Moroccan mint for teas. Apple mint has a wonderfully soft flavour and is the most readily expansive, covering ground rapidly. Spearmint 'Kentucky Colonel' is traditionally used in mint juleps and mojitos. You could also try Bowles mint for jellies and sauces.

STARTING OFF: Source plants from a good supplier or propagate from established plants by digging up a section of root that has some stalk attached, and potting up.

POSITION: Mints like a very moist soil and sun or partial shade. They grow well in deep containers, which will also keep their spreading growth in check.

SPACING: Plants spread irregularly.

PRODUCTIVITY/EFFICIENCY: Effortless: once planted, you'll never be without it.

GROWING: Cut back to the ground in winter and give an occasional mulch of compost or manure. Don't grow different mints next to each other, as they lose their distinctiveness if their roots intertwine.

POTENTIAL PROBLEMS: Generally pest and disease free.

HARVEST: Pick stems and leaves as required throughout the growing season.

MYRTLE

Myrtus communis. Also known as: common myrtle. Half-hardy evergreen.

A fantastic herb that produces well all year round (I find it especially useful in winter) and with wonderful berries that I use in place of juniper. Its scent and flavour are fairly similar to juniper but there is also some of the bright generosity of bay. And, as with both juniper and bay, myrtle imparts itself beautifully when burned on the barbecue or in a smoker. Myrtle and meat – red or white – were made for each other.

VARIETIES: You could also try the small-leaved *M. communis* subsp. *tarentina*.

STARTING OFF: Source plants from a good nursery.

POSITION: Although half-hardy it will grow very well in a sunny, sheltered, free-draining spot. Growing in a pot is ideal as you can bring it indoors for the winter.

SPACING: Can reach 3m in width, though usually stays smaller.

PRODUCTIVITY/EFFICIENCY: A small evergreen shrub with plentiful leaves, requiring little input.

GROWING: Very little required apart from the occasional mulch with compost.

POTENTIAL PROBLEMS: Generally pest and disease free.

HARVEST: Pick new leaves from spring through to autumn, and

pick not too heavily over winter or dry some leaves in midsummer to use through the cold months. Fruit can be harvested in autumn.

NASTURTIUM

Tropaeolum majus. Half-hardy annual.

I can't think of a single reason why any garden would be without nasturtiums. Their fabulously fairy tale flowers are abundantly borne throughout the growing season, looking a treat, drawing in bees, and they are one of the finest edible flowers. If you've yet to experience them, pop one in your mouth whole: their first flavour is of rocket, becoming more honeyed as you reach the nectar, ending in a flourish of pepper. The young leaves are similarly fine – a fresh brassica flavour with gentle pepper, superb in salads or as the base for a risotto. As fast-growing ground cover, an effective companion plant and a weed-suppressing self-sower, it will be a hard-working part of your garden too.

VARIETIES: Try the dark foliage of 'Empress of India' or the deep red flowers of 'Black Velvet'. 'Moonlight' has pretty primrose-coloured flowers and 'Alaska' has variegated leaves.

STARTING OFF: Sow seed in modules under cover from April and plant out after the last frosts.

POSITION: Nasturtiums flower best in poor soil but like some moisture. Ideal for containers.

SPACING: 15–30cm apart.

PRODUCTIVITY/EFFICIENCY: A very productive crop over the summer and early autumn months, with leaves, flowers and young seed pods all being edible. Self-seeds if allowed.

GROWING: Water whilst establishing.

POTENTIAL PROBLEMS: Pinch out parts affected by blackfly.

HARVEST: Pick young leaves, flowers and seed as required.

PARSLEY

Petroselinum crispum and *P. crispum* var. *neapolitanum*. Also known as: garden parsley, and Italian and flat-leaved parsley respectively. Hardy biennial, grown as an annual.

I use parsley more days than not, but heavens above: let me not see it ever again as an unwanted 'garnish' on anything from a cooked breakfast to a beef Wellington. Parsley is simply too good to become the ubiquitous, undervalued bit of greenery. I'll take a pesto of parsley over basil any day, and gremolata (a blend of garlic, lemon zest and parsley) brings out the best in fish, prawns, potatoes and lamb. I tend to use the curly, slightly coarser, bolder parsley when adding it late to cooking, and the flat-leaved variety for using raw. Try a handful of small leaves in a mixed salad.

VARIETIES: Few named varieties available.

STARTING OFF: A sowing in spring and in mid- and late summer should last you year-long. Sow seed in modules under cover, planting out when the roots are showing.

POSITION: A sunny spot with rich, moist soil. It will also do well in containers.

SPACING: 20cm apart.

PRODUCTIVITY/EFFICIENCY: With three sowings you can have year-round parsley for very little effort – a very productive cut-and-come-again herb.

GROWING: Keep soil moist during dry weather. Protect winter plants with a cloche or fleece.

POTENTIAL PROBLEMS: Plant near onions and garlic to deter carrot fly.

HARVEST: Pick leaves as required but only use them in the first year – those in the plant's second year won't be so good as it gets ready to flower.

PERILLA

Perilla frutescens. Also known as: shiso. Half-hardy annual.

A peculiarly, inexplicably unknown herb with a flavour between cumin and mint: more of the latter when the weather is cool; the former dominating in the heat. Shredded and added late to soups, pasta and fish dishes it brings a little of both of those fine flavours, but I think I love it most when it is more upfront, in pesto and to bring out the best in aubergines. Perilla comes in green and deep purple varieties, equally beautiful, and with a floppy-leaved habit, a little like a lazy, crinkle-edged mint.

VARIETIES: There are green and purple forms of perilla.

STARTING OFF: Sow seed in modules under cover in April and again in June or July. Pot on and plant out after the danger of frosts has passed.

POSITION: A sunny spot in moist, rich soil. Perilla will also grow well in pots.

SPACING: 30cm apart.

PRODUCTIVITY/EFFICIENCY: Perilla makes bushy plants with lots of leaves for use throughout the summer and early autumn.

GROWING: Keep soil moist and pinch out tips to make bushy plants.

POTENTIAL PROBLEMS: Generally pest and disease free.

HARVEST: Pick leaves as needed, and use the flowers as a lively garnish or tossed through salads.

ROSE

HEDGEROW ROSE

Rosa rugosa. Also known as: apple rose. Hardy perennial shrub.

Many roses are good for eating in one form or another, but to my mind *Rosa rugosa* tops the lot. A great hedging plant, it also works well when allowed to form a relaxed clump in the corner of the garden. *R. rugosa* is the rose for syrups, jellies and fruit salads, being full of scent and flavour. Its large, loose, informal petals waft about in the lightest breeze, easily separating from the plant with a gentle pull. My daughter likes me to throw a handful into her running bath water to fill it with scent and colour. The hips make a fine jelly and a fabulous jam. But perhaps most pleasingly, a handful or two of petals in a jar filled with vodka makes the most amazing infusion.

VARIETIES: You could try 'Rubra' for its magenta flowers or 'Alba' for its white ones. 'Scabrosa' reputedly has larger flowers and fruit.

STARTING OFF: Source plants from a good supplier or propagate from suckers.

POSITION: Happy in most soils including poor ones. Plant in sun or partial shade.

SPACING: Can reach 1.5m high and wide. Space at 60cm–1m if planting as an edible hedge.

PRODUCTIVITY/EFFICIENCY: *Rosa rugosa* flowers generously throughout the summer and autumn, followed by large hips that can also be harvested over a long period. Once planted it can be left to fend for itself.

GROWING: An occasional mulch of compost will be appreciated but is by no means essential.

POTENTIAL PROBLEMS: One of the most disease-resistant roses. They are generally pest free too.

HARVEST: Pick petals when the flowers are fully open, and hips when orangey red and just beginning to soften.

ROSEMARY

Rosmarinus officinalis. Hardy evergreen.

Lamb and potatoes, roasted, are almost impossible to imagine without the resinous loveliness of rosemary to colour them with flavour. This essentially woody herb needs a well-drained soil to be at its best - give it that and a sunny spot and it'll throw long sprigs (think a sparsely leaved Christmas tree branch) upwards all year round. A deep, warming, homely scent and flavour that's as good with fish and roasted vegetables as it is with lamb.

VARIETIES: Try 'Miss Jessop's Upright', which does as it says, or 'Alba' for white flowers. You could also try 'Corsica Prostratus' whose creeping habit can cause it to cascade down the side of a raised bed.

STARTING OFF: Source plants of named varieties from a good supplier or propagate from semi-ripe cuttings in late summer.

POSITION: Full sun and shelter in a soil with very good drainage.

SPACING: 1.5m apart.

PRODUCTIVITY/EFFICIENCY: Once established, rosemary makes a maintenance-free plant which will provide you with a year-round harvest.

GROWING: Water whilst establishing and avoid picking while it reaches a nice size. Over-picking means the plant never gets a chance to reach a good productive size.

POTENTIAL PROBLEMS: If you find the beautiful rosemary beetle, hold an upturned umbrella beneath the plant and give the branches a shake, disposing of the beetles as you will. Generally disease free.

HARVEST: Snip stems off as required throughout the year.

SAGE

Salvia officinalis. Hardy evergreen perennial.

One of the 'love it or loathe it' herbs that seems to split a room. I'm in the 'love it' camp: though I don't use it often, I wouldn't be without it. Its lively camphorous, warming spiciness was made to go with pork, squash and veal. It is also a worthy addition to beans and, somewhat weirdly, apples, too. A great herb for drying – just cut and hang in the kitchen to use when suits.

VARIETIES: Purple 'Purpurascens' is beautiful and no less delicious than the traditional green variety, or try 'Icterina' for a variegated form.

STARTING OFF: Source plants of named varieties from a good supplier or propagate from softwood cuttings in spring or semi-hardwood cuttings in late summer. The generic form and 'Purpurascens' can both be raised from seed. Sow seed in spring in modules under cover, potting on once before planting out.

POSITION: Full sun or part-shade in soil with good drainage. Some shelter would be appreciated and plants will happily grow in pots.

SPACING: Can reach 1m in width and height.

PRODUCTIVITY/EFFICIENCY: A maintenance-free plant that will provide you with year-round sage.

GROWING: Cut back hard in spring to encourage fresh young leaves. Replace plants every 5 years or so when they become woody and sparse.

POTENTIAL PROBLEMS: Generally untroubled by pests and diseases.

HARVEST: Harvest leaves as required. Also pick the flowers in early summer for adding to a salad.

SALAD BURNET

Sanguisorba minor. Also known as: garden burnet. Hardy perennial.

A herb that's crept up on me in the last decade, and I now find I'm looking for excuses to use it at any opportunity. A hardy, year-round feature in the garden, salad burnet's oval, shark tooth-edged leaves carry the same cool, fresh flavour as cucumber. In spring, the young new growth is succulent enough to take its place in a leafy salad, acting more as a herb as the leaves become less tender in the summer. A handful in a jug of water lends it glorious refreshment – and it should be compulsory for all lovers of Pimm's.

VARIETIES: Usually sold in its generic form.

STARTING OFF: Source plants or sow seed in modules in spring or autumn, potting on once before planting out. You can also divide established plants.

POSITION: Full sun or partial shade in well-drained soil. It does very well in containers.

SPACING: 30cm apart.

PRODUCTIVITY/EFFICIENCY: Fresh young leaves can be picked throughout the growing season (and sometimes through the winter) year on year and with little maintenance.

GROWING: Cut back flower stems to promote fresh leafy growth.

POTENTIAL PROBLEMS: Generally pest and disease free.

HARVEST: Pick young leaves for eating raw before flowering. Coarser leaves can be picked for cooking.

SCENTED PELARGONIUMS

Pelargonium species. Half-hardy perennial.

I can't be doing with regular geraniums – I find their scent really off-putting – but scented pelargoniums (call them 'geraniums' and expect a brolly around the head from specialist growers) are something else entirely. If all you do is take a handful of leaves from 'Attar of Roses' and make a syrup for drizzling over cakes, ice cream and cocktails, you'll be convinced enough to grow them every year. Its fragrance and flavour are a must for home-made Turkish delight too. There are many different flavours and scents to try – lime, orange and chocolate amongst them.

VARIETIES: There are many and with a range of scents. Some that stand out are 'Attar of Roses' with its Turkish delight rose scent; 'Orange Fizz' with a lemon sherbet/orange scent, pretty flowers and an upright habit; and 'Pink Capitatum' with lime-scented leaves and fabulous mauve/pink flowers.

STARTING OFF: Source plants of a named variety from a specialist supplier (remembering to call them 'scented pelargoniums') or take cuttings in late summer.

POSITION: They need sun and a free-draining soil. Being tender, they are best grown in pots so they can be brought indoors for the winter.

SPACING: Grow in a roomy container.

PRODUCTIVITY/EFFICIENCY: Easy to grow and full of flavour and scent, perfect for container growing and adaptable to many recipes. In leaf from spring to early autumn. One established plant of each variety is usually plenty, as leaves replenish quickly.

GROWING: Feed every couple of weeks with a comfrey tea or tomato feed. One for growing in containers, so you can bring plants indoors over winter as they are vulnerable to the cold.

POTENTIAL PROBLEMS: Generally pest and disease free.

HARVEST: Pick leaves as required from mid-spring into autumn.

SUMMER SAVORY

Satureja hortensis. Hardy annual.

A very under-appreciated herb with a flavour and fragrance like a slightly minty, piney oregano. Substantial but not heavy, its flavour works beautifully with dairy, chicken and fish and with most vegetables, especially when cooking tomatoes. I tend to use the leaves and stems during cooking, but when the leaves are fresh and light, they work equally well added as you might parsley.

VARIETIES: Generic.

STARTING OFF: Sow seed in modules from spring, planting out when roots are showing. Make several sowings for a continual supply.

POSITION: Full sun in a well-drained soil and will do well in a container.

SPACING: 20cm apart.

PRODUCTIVITY/EFFICIENCY: A low-maintenance, hardy herb that's big on flavour.

GROWING: Cut back flowering stems to encourage leafy growth and prolong its productive life.

POTENTIAL PROBLEMS: Generally pest and disease free.

HARVEST: Pick leaves and stems as required between May and September.

SWEET CICELY

Myrrhis odorata. Also known as: anise and garden myrrh. Hardy perennial.

I am rather overly attached to sweet cicely. It comes out bright and thrusting in early spring with fern-like leaves of the sweetest aniseed, perfectly timed to accompany its natural partner, the first of the rhubarb. The gentle aniseed lessens the sharpness of the rhubarb, which means you can use less sugar than you might otherwise, and it brings out the flavour of the stalks beautifully. The baton-shaped seeds, often formed as early as late spring, are delicious too – try them in biscuits, stir-fries and spice mixes. It grows happily in a pot and is one of those very handy plants that loves half-shade and will tolerate fairly full-on shade.

VARIETIES: Generic.

STARTING OFF: Source plants from a good supplier or grow from seed. Seed need a prolonged period of cold to germinate so are best sown in situ in autumn. You could also try mixing them with damp compost in a plastic bag and placing in the fridge for several weeks before sowing in pots in spring. Seed is only viable for a year, so ensure it is fresh.

POSITION: Likes a partially shady spot in rich, moist but well-draining soil. It has deep taproots so won't do well in a pot.

SPACING: 40cm apart.

PRODUCTIVITY/EFFICIENCY: Sweet cicely will give you fresh leaves for a good part of the year and the roots and seeds can also be eaten. It is worth having more than one plant if you wish to use both fresh leaves and seeds.

GROWING: Cut back after flowering to increase fresh leaf production.

POTENTIAL PROBLEMS: Generally untroubled by pests and diseases.

HARVEST: Leaves can be harvested throughout the growing season. Collect seeds whilst still green to use fresh. Roots can be dug up in winter to eat and will store well in sand for several months, but I tend to leave them in situ and harvest just seeds and leaves.

SZECHUAN PEPPER

Zanthoxylum species. Deciduous shrub.

My desert island spice, without question. The harshly pink/red peppercorns in autumn are full of both peppery wallop and a peculiar tingly numbing sensation that affects the tongue and lips, as well as causing a rush of salivation and hunger. It is quite something. The combination of pepperiness and its numbing qualities makes it the core ingredient in Chinese five spice and a real treat with anything hot and salty - squid, chips or onion rings are my favourite. The leaves carry much of the scent and flavour but without the tingle; I pick them in spring while they are tiny for salads, and later to work their way into mayonnaise and sauces. Picked early, while still green, the peppercorns are perhaps even livelier, though they dry less well at this stage and so should be used fresh.

VARIETIES: *Z. schinifolium* and *Z. simulans* but you could also try *Z. armatum* (a Nepalese pepper) and *Z. piperitum* (a Japanese pepper). Self-fertile but may give heavier yields with another bush for pollination.

STARTING OFF: Source plants from a specialist supplier, as germination from seed is tricky and erratic.

POSITION: Happy in most soils but likes the sun.

SPACING: Over time can reach many metres in height and spread if allowed to, but can be pruned to a smaller size and for container growing.

PRODUCTIVITY/EFFICIENCY: Szechuan peppers begin to bear fruit in their third or fourth year and quickly become very productive. The very young leaves are really good in early spring salads. Once established, they'll ask for none of your attention.

GROWING: Little maintenance required, just pruning for size whenever you feel the need.

POTENTIAL PROBLEMS: Generally pest and disease free, although keep away from citrus trees as Szechuan peppers can (though rarely do) carry a hard-to-treat canker that affects citrus plants.

HARVEST: Pick entire heads when the outer shells begin to split revealing the dark seed inside. This can be any time from October to December depending on the weather. Dry for a few days in the warmth and remove the stems before storing. Peppercorns freeze well too, keeping their flavour for longer.

TASMANIAN MOUNTAIN PEPPER

Drimys lanceolata (syn. *Tasmannia lanceolata*). Also known as: Australian pepper and Cornish pepper leaf. Evergreen shrub.

An evergreen that is borderline hardy, so therefore needs a sheltered, sunny spot to thrive and produce its lively berries that can be dried and used as pepper. Given its requirements, this is a great plant for growing in an urban situation where the microclimate is likely to suit it well compared with more exposed situations. They're very happy to be clipped to form a hedge if required.

VARIETIES: Male and female flowers are borne on separate plants so you will need one of each for the female to produce berries.

STARTING OFF: Source plants from a specialist supplier.

POSITION: Fertile, moist and well-drained soil. Happy in sun or part-shade but needs shelter to do well.

SPACING: 2.5m wide and 4m high.

PRODUCTIVITY/EFFICIENCY: Its peppery seeds are produced in generous quantities and the plant needs little attention to produce year after year.

GROWING: Prune for shape as required.

POTENTIAL PROBLEMS: Generally pest and disease free.

HARVEST: Berries are ready in autumn, and the leaves can be picked for tea all year. Use fresh or spread out to dry in a greenhouse or polytunnel for a few days.

THYME

Thymus vulgaris. Hardy evergreen perennial.

I need to have quite a few plants of this on the go to keep up with my consumption, lending its fragrant, smoky intensity to red and white meat, fish, soups too numerous to mention and roasted vegetables. If you haven't the space to grow enough for your needs, buy it, as the plants suffer when over-cropped – you can always dedicate the space to lemon and orange thyme.

Both are truly splendid, adding their citrus vim to the thyme's depth. I use both in cocktails, fruit salads, on pizza, and in milk puddings – crème brûlée infused with either is heaven.

VARIETIES: Broad-leaved thyme (*T. pulegioides*) is one of the best culinary thymes. Also try lemon thyme (*T. citriodorus*) or orange thyme ('Fragrantissimus').

STARTING OFF: Source plants from a good supplier. Some thymes, such as *T. vulgaris* and 'Fragrantissimus', can also be started by seed. Sow seed in modules in spring and pot on until large enough to be planted outside.

POSITION: Thrives in poor, free-draining soil and is ideal for growing in pots.

SPACING: Up to 50cm apart, depending on variety.

PRODUCTIVITY/EFFICIENCY: As an evergreen, thyme can be harvested for use throughout the year. Grow more than one so you don't cut back too much into hardwood, as thyme, like lavender, doesn't like this.

GROWING: Cut back after flowering – not too far into old wood – to encourage fresh growth.

POTENTIAL PROBLEMS: Generally pest and disease free but can be short-lived in the UK's wet weather.

HARVEST: Pick tender young stems and flowers for use in spring and summer, and tougher stems in winter for use in stocks and stews.

TURKISH ROCKET

Bunias orientalis. Also known as: warty cabbage. Hardy perennial.

A really flavoursome perennial vegetable despite its rather unappetising alternative name. Don't let it put you off. It resembles a vast dandelion crossed with cime di rapa. The leaves and miniature broccoli heads both carry a punchy, mustard greens flavour that is superb treated as a spicy green vegetable or used raw, early in the season when it is tender.

VARIETIES: Usually available only in its generic form.

STARTING OFF: Source plants from a specialist supplier, propagate by division in spring or start from seed. Sow seed in March or April in modules under cover. Pot on once and plant out once the roots are showing.

POSITION: Full sun or part-shade in most reasonably drained soils.

SPACING: 45cm apart.

PRODUCTIVITY/EFFICIENCY: A vigorous and resilient plant that provides you with crops from late winter/early spring until autumn.

GROWING: Hardy, drought resistant and reliable, with little maintenance required.

POTENTIAL PROBLEMS: Slugs like the young growth but it usually grows quickly enough to outgrow their attentions.

HARVEST: Pick young leaves in early spring for eating raw, and older leaves throughout the growing season for cooking as you would spinach. You can also eat the flower stems and broccoli-like flower buds, which appear in summer, raw or lightly cooked.

WATERCRESS

Nasturtium officinale. Hardy perennial.

A wonderfully punchy, peppery leaf that has been popular here since Roman times. It is usually commercially grown in running water, but will thrive in a good deep soil instead. Rich in vitamins and minerals, watercress is delicious as a salad leaf or when cooked.

VARIETIES: Usually available only in its generic form.

STARTING OFF: Source plants or seed from a specialist supplier. Sow seed in pots or trays that are then immersed to half their depth in water. Pot on once before planting out.

POSITION: Likes slow-flowing, clean water or moist soil. Equally happy planted in the shallows of a pond or in a pot. Happy in sun or a reasonable amount of shade.

SPACING: Has a spreading habit, and tends to knit together into a fine edible ground cover when planted at around 10–20cm apart.

PRODUCTIVITY/EFFICIENCY: Watercress has a long cropping season and needs little attention once established.

GROWING: Little maintenance needed, other than maintaining a moist environment.

POTENTIAL PROBLEMS: Generally pest and disease free.

HARVEST: Pick leaves and stems throughout the growing season.

WELSH ONION

Allium fistulosum. Also known as: Japanese bunching onion. Hardy perennial.

A really striking, handsome onion that in many ways is more like a musclebound variety of chives. The hollow stems can grow wide and substantial if allowed, but if regularly cut they stay just slightly larger than most chives. Left to grow, they'll produce flower heads, somewhere between chives and leeks in size and flavour. All parts are delicious raw or cooked, used in recipes as you would chives or leeks.

VARIETIES: This is a multiplier type of onion and is available in its generic form.

STARTING OFF: Source plants from a good supplier or propagate by dividing established clumps. Welsh onions also grow easily from seed. Sow in modules under cover in spring, and plant out when the roots are showing, or sow direct from April.

POSITION: Full sun or partial shade in a good, well-drained soil.

SPACING: 50cm apart.

PRODUCTIVITY/EFFICIENCY: Stems, leaves and flowers are all edible in this traditional cottage garden plant. It is of particular use when storage onions have come to an end and new-season onions are not yet ready.

GROWING: Allow plants to establish before harvesting stems and leaves. Cut back to the ground after flowering to encourage fresh new growth.

POTENTIAL PROBLEMS: Generally pest and disease free.

HARVEST: Leaves grow back quickly and you can make several cuttings so use the leaves as you would spring onions during the growing season. You can also lift whole stems throughout the growing season. While the plants are flowering, the stems won't be good to eat but the flowers themselves are edible.

WILD GARLIC

Allium ursinum. Also known as: ramson and wood garlic. Hardy perennial.

Living in the South West, wild garlic pops its nose up earlier than in most parts of the country, perhaps by mid-February, although we usually wait until March to start taking the first leaves. Check your nearest woods, as it loves the dappled shade and moist conditions of beech trees, though some grows on the riverbank that runs around our smallholding too. If there's no local source, it's easy to grow in your garden. Try to replicate its favoured shady, damp conditions to get it at its best. Risottos, ravioli, pesto, omelettes and breakfast scrambled eggs are all likely to be lifted by its gentle garlicky presence throughout the spring.

VARIETIES: Available in its generic form only. You could also try the three-cornered leek (*A. triquetrum*) or daffodil garlic (*A. neapolitanum*), both of which complement wild garlic by producing edible leaves from autumn to spring.

STARTING OFF: Buy young plants from a good supplier or sow seed directly in a damp, shady spot from June to autumn.

POSITION: A damp, humus-rich soil in a shady spot.

SPACING: 30cm apart.

PRODUCTIVITY/EFFICIENCY: Happiest in the shady damp where few plants thrive, it can produce an abundant crop for around 3 months of the year. Can be left completely to its own devices.

GROWING: No maintenance required other than weeding if growing in the garden.

POTENTIAL PROBLEMS: Generally pest and disease free.

HARVEST: Pick leaves from March to May as well as flowers.

WINTER SAVORY

Satureja montana. Hardy semi-evergreen perennial.

Not a million miles away in flavour and fragrance from its summer relative, winter savory has perhaps more menthol, thyme and pepperiness to it. It packs an altogether more powerful punch, perfect for winter recipes that require a bit of presence – just go easy though, as it can dominate.

VARIETIES: Generic.

STARTING OFF: Source plants from a good supplier or grow from seed. Sow seed in modules in early spring but don't cover, as the seed needs light to germinate.

POSITION: Tolerant of most soils but must have good drainage and full sun. Winter savory grows well in a pot.

SPACING: 50cm apart.

PRODUCTIVITY/EFFICIENCY: Particularly valuable in the garden in warmer parts of the country where it can remain evergreen, offering structure during winter as well as its wonderful flavour.

GROWING: Cut back after flowering to promote fresh new growth.

POTENTIAL PROBLEMS: Generally pest and disease free.

HARVEST: Cut stems and leaves as required in the growing season and more conservatively in winter.

GROWING CHARTS

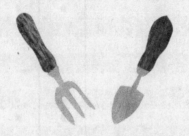

Use these growing charts to help prioritise
what makes it into your kitchen garden.
The year-long guide gives an idea of
when to expect to harvest each food.

VEGETABLES	JAN	FEB	MAR	APR	
AGRETTI				●	
ASPARAGUS				●	
AUBERGINES					
BAMBOO				●	
BEETROOT					
BORLOTTI BEANS					
BROAD BEANS				●	
BRUSSELS SPROUTS	●	●	●	●	
BUCK'S HORN PLANTAIN				●	
CABBAGE	●	●	●	●	
CALABRESE					
CALLALOO					
CARDOONS					
CARROTS					
CAULIFLOWER	●	●	●	●	
CELERIAC	●	●	●		
CELERY					
CHARD & PERPETUAL SPINACH	●	●	●	●	
CHERVIL & PARSLEY ROOT	●	●	●	●	
CHICORY	●				
CHILLI PEPPERS					
CHINESE ARTICHOKE	●	●			
CHINESE CEDAR				●	
CHOP SUEY GREENS					
CIME DI RAPA					
COURGETTES (inc. flowers)					
CUCAMELONS					
CUCUMBERS & GHERKINS					
DAUBENTON'S KALE	●	●	●	●	
DAYLILIES				●	
EARTH CHESTNUT					

MAY	JUN	JUL	AUG	SEP	OCT	NOV	DEC
•	•	•	•	•	•		
•							
			•	•	•		
•	•	•	•	•	•		
		•	•	•	•		
			•	•	•		
•	•	•	•	•			
					•	•	•
•	•						
•	•	•	•	•	•	•	•
	•	•	•	•			
	•	•	•	•			
					•	•	
•	•	•	•	•	•	•	
•	•	•	•	•	•	•	•
				•	•	•	•
		•	•	•	•		
•	•	•	•	•	•	•	•
•	•	•	•	•	•	•	•
					•	•	•
			•	•	•		
					•	•	•
•	•	•					
•	•	•	•	•	•		
•	•	•	•	•	•		
	•	•	•	•	•		
		•	•	•			
	•	•	•	•	•		
•	•	•	•	•	•	•	•
•	•	•	•	•			
•	•	•	•	•	•	•	

VEGETABLES	JAN	FEB	MAR	APR
EGYPTIAN WALKING ONION	●	●	●	●
ENDIVE	●	●	●	
FLORENCE FENNEL				
FRENCH BEANS				
GARLIC				●
GARLIC CRESS	●	●	●	●
GARLIC MUSTARD				●
GLOBE ARTICHOKES				
GOOD KING HENRY				●
GROUND NUT	●	●		
HOPS				●
HOSTA			●	●
JERUSALEM ARTICHOKES	●	●		
KAI LÁN				
KALE	●	●		
KOHLRABI				
LEEKS	●	●	●	●
LETTUCE	●	●	●	●
MASHUA				
MEXICAN TREE SPINACH				●
MIBUNA	●	●	●	●
MICROLEAVES	●	●	●	●
MIZUNA	●	●	●	●
MOOLI				
MUSHROOMS	●	●	●	●
NEW ZEALAND SPINACH				●
OCA				
ONIONS				
OSTRICH FERN			●	●
PARSNIPS	●	●	●	
PEAS				

MAY	JUN	JUL	AUG	SEP	OCT	NOV	DEC
•	•	•	•	•	•	•	•
			•	•	•	•	•
		•	•	•	•	•	
	•	•	•	•	•		
•	•	•					
•				•	•	•	•
•	•	•	•				
•	•	•	•				
•	•	•	•	•			
					•	•	•
•	•			•	•		
					•	•	•
•	•		•	•	•		
	•	•	•	•	•	•	•
	•	•	•	•	•		
•				•	•	•	•
•	•	•	•	•	•	•	•
	•	•	•	•	•	•	•
•	•	•	•	•			
•	•	•	•	•	•	•	•
•	•	•	•	•	•	•	•
•	•	•	•	•	•	•	•
			•	•	•	•	
•	•	•	•	•	•	•	•
•	•	•	•	•			
					•	•	
•	•	•	•				
•							
			•	•	•	•	•
•	•	•	•	•			

VEGETABLES	JAN	FEB	MAR	APR	
POTATOES (non-maincrop)					
POTATOES (maincrop)					
PURSLANE (winter & summer)	●	●	●	●	
QUINOA					
RADISH				●	
RED VALERIAN	●	●	●	●	
ROCKET				●	
ROMANESCO	●				
RUNNER BEANS					
SALSIFY & SCORZONERA	●	●			
SEA KALE	●	●	●	●	
SHALLOTS					
SIBERIAN PEA TREE					
SMALL-LEAVED LIME				●	
SOCIETY GARLIC					
SOLOMON'S SEAL				●	
SORREL					
SPINACH	●	●	●	●	
SPRING ONIONS			●	●	
SPROUTING BROCCOLI	●	●	●	●	
SQUASH					
STINGING NETTLES			●	●	
SWEDE					
SWEETCORN					
SWEET PEPPERS					
SWEET POTATO					
TOMATILLOS					
TOMATOES					
TURNIPS					
VIOLA 'HEARTSEASE'				●	
YACON					

MAY	JUN	JUL	AUG	SEP	OCT	NOV	DEC
•	•	•					
			•	•	•		
•	•	•	•	•	•	•	•
				•	•		
•	•	•	•	•	•	•	
•	•	•	•	•	•	•	•
			•	•	•	•	•
	•	•	•	•	•		
					•	•	•
•						•	•
		•	•				
	•	•					
•	•						
•	•	•	•	•			
•							
•	•	•	•	•	•	•	
•	•	•	•	•	•	•	•
•	•	•	•	•	•	•	
				•	•		
•							
				•	•	•	•
		•	•	•	•		
		•	•	•	•		
					•	•	•
		•	•	•	•		
		•	•	•	•		
•	•	•	•	•	•	•	•
•	•	•	•	•	•	•	
					•	•	

FRUIT & NUTS	JAN	FEB	MAR	APR	
ALMONDS					
ALPINE STRAWBERRIES					
APPLES					
APRICOTS					
ASIAN PEARS					
AUTUMN OLIVE					
BLACKBERRIES					
BLACKCURRANTS					
BLUE BEAN					
BLUEBERRIES					
BLUE HONEYSUCKLE					
BOYSENBERRIES					
CAPE GOOSEBERRIES					
CHERRIES					
CHILEAN GUAVA					
CHOCOLATE VINE					
CRANBERRIES					
ELDER					
FIGS					
FUCHSIA					
GOJI BERRIES					
GOOSEBERRIES					
GRAPES (inc. leaves)					
HAWTHORN					
HAZEL					
JAPANESE PLUMS					
JAPANESE QUINCE					
JAPANESE WINEBERRIES					
JOSTABERRY					
JUNEBERRY					
KIWIS					

MAY	JUN	JUL	AUG	SEP	OCT	NOV	DEC
●	●				●	●	
●	●	●	●	●			
		●	●	●	●	●	●
		●	●	●			
		●	●	●	●		
				●	●	●	
		●	●	●	●		
	●	●	●	●			
				●	●		
		●	●	●			
●	●						
		●	●	●			
		●	●	●	●	●	
		●	●	●			
					●	●	
				●			
			●	●	●		
●	●	●	●	●	●	●	
			●	●			
		●	●	●			
		●	●	●	●		
●	●	●					
	●	●	●	●	●		
				●	●		
				●	●	●	●
		●					
				●	●	●	
		●	●	●			
	●	●					
	●	●					
				●	●	●	●

FRUIT & NUTS	JAN	FEB	MAR	APR	
LINGONBERRY					
MEDLAR					
MELONS					
MIRABELLE PLUMS					
MULBERRIES (inc. leaves)					
NEPALESE RASPBERRIES					
OLIVES	●				
PEACHES & NECTARINES					
PEARS					
PECANS					
PINEAPPLE GUAVA					
PLUMS, DAMSONS & GAGES					
QUINCE					
RASPBERRIES					
REDCURRANTS & WHITE CURRANTS					
RHUBARB (inc. forced)		●	●	●	
SCHISANDRA					
SEA BUCKTHORN					
STRAWBERRIES					
SWEET CHESTNUTS					
WALNUTS (inc. green walnuts)					
WORCESTERBERRIES					

	MAY	JUN	JUL	AUG	SEP	OCT	NOV	DEC
			●	●	●			
						●	●	
				●	●	●		
			●	●	●			
				●	●			
			●	●				
						●	●	●
			●	●				
				●	●	●	●	
						●	●	
			●		●	●	●	
			●	●	●			
						●		
			●	●	●	●	●	
			●	●				
	●	●	●					
				●	●			
				●	●	●		
	●	●	●	●	●	●	●	
						●	●	
		●	●		●	●	●	
			●	●				

HERBS & SPICES	JAN	FEB	MAR	APR	
ANGELICA					
ANISE HYSSOP					
BABINGTON'S LEEK	●	●	●		
BASIL					
BAY	●	●	●	●	
BERGAMOT				●	
BORAGE				●	
CARAWAY					
CAROLINA ALLSPICE					
CELERY LEAF	●	●	●	●	
CHERVIL	●	●	●	●	
CHIVES				●	
CORIANDER					
DILL					
ENGLISH MACE				●	
FENNEL					
FENUGREEK					
FRENCH TARRAGON					
HORSERADISH	●	●	●	●	
HYSSOP	●	●	●	●	
JAPANESE PARSLEY	●	●	●	●	
LAVENDER					
LEMON BALM				●	
LEMONGRASS					
LEMON VERBENA					
LOVAGE				●	
MARIGOLD					
MARJORAM & OREGANO					
MINT				●	
MYRTLE	●	●	●	●	
NASTURTIUM					

MAY	JUN	JUL	AUG	SEP	OCT	NOV	DEC
	●	●	●	●			
●	●	●	●	●			
			●			●	●
	●	●	●	●			
●	●	●	●	●	●	●	●
●	●	●	●	●			
●	●	●	●	●	●		
●	●	●	●				
		●	●				
●	●	●	●	●	●	●	●
●	●	●	●	●	●	●	●
●	●	●	●	●	●		
●	●	●	●	●	●		
●	●	●	●	●	●		
●	●	●	●	●	●		
●	●	●	●	●	●		
●	●	●	●	●			
●	●	●	●	●			
●	●	●	●	●	●	●	●
●	●	●	●	●	●	●	●
●	●	●	●	●	●	●	●
●	●	●					
●	●	●	●	●			
●	●	●	●	●	●		
●	●	●	●	●	●		
●	●	●	●	●	●	●	
●	●	●	●	●	●		
●	●	●	●	●	●		
●	●	●	●	●	●		
●	●	●	●	●	●	●	●
●	●	●	●	●			

HERBS & SPICES	JAN	FEB	MAR	APR
PARSLEY				
PERILLA				
ROSE (HEDGEROW)				
ROSEMARY	●	●	●	●
SAGE	●	●	●	●
SALAD BURNET	●	●	●	●
SCENTED PELARGONIUMS				
SUMMER SAVORY				
SWEET CICELY				●
SZECHUAN PEPPER				●
TASMANIAN MOUNTAIN PEPPER	●	●	●	●
THYME	●	●	●	●
TURKISH ROCKET				●
WATERCRESS				●
WELSH ONION	●	●	●	●
WILD GARLIC	●	●	●	●
WINTER SAVORY	●	●	●	●